The Ways of Friendship

The Ways

of Friendship

Ignace Lepp

Translated by BERNARD MURCHLAND

THE MACMILLAN COMPANY, NEW YORK

Contents

Foreword

IN THE course of my career as a writer—already a long one—I have often treated themes that were altogether new; at other times I have written on topics that few writers had touched upon previously. This is not the case in the present book. As a matter of fact, the theme of friendship has been extensively treated by many writers and thinkers. Homer spoke of it in his *Odyssey*. Plato and Xenophon tell us that Socrates often discussed friendship with his disciples. Cicero, Seneca, Horace, Ovid and many other celebrated writers in Greco-Roman times have either written whole books about friendship or discoursed upon it in important parts of one or another of their works. This is also true of the early Christian and medieval writers. Closer to us, Montaigne, Shakespeare and many other authors have praised friendship while Nietzsche, Schopenhauer and their followers have doubted its possibility.

But not all of these authors have understood friendship to be the same psychological or emotional reality. For those in the Socratic tradition friendship meant primarily an intense intellectual communion. Christian writers understood it principally as communion with God. For others the term is equivalent to something like "combat camaraderie," while the Romantics, following Rousseau, emphasize sentimental effusiveness. Today we say "my dear friend" to all and sundry, to the point that the word has lost all concrete meaning.

If, following in the footsteps of such illustrious writers, I propose to analyze and develop once again the theme of friendship, it is because it has played an important role in my own life and I should like to acquit myself of a debt toward it. In my youth it was because of friendship that I experienced the deepest and purest joys which enabled me to overcome the many obstacles in the path of my career. If today, at a mature age, I continue to believe in man and to trust in the future of humanity, I am convinced that I am still indebted to my friends for this belief. Also, my long practice as a depth psychologist has enabled me to verify the important role friendship can play in promoting authentic existence and to observe the distress of those who are deprived of it. Thus, I also hope that this book will be a practical one.

I had at first planned, when one of my publishing friends asked me to write a book on friendship, to compose a work in the poetic vein and thus celebrate the sublime beauties of friendship. But as the book progressed it became increasingly clear that I ought to treat such an important subject in my capacity as a psychologist and pedagogue. That is why I make extensive use of my personal experience and of the experience of those who have confided in me. This will not be a scholarly book. I am convinced that friendship is one of the most fundamental of existential values, that it can make man's life infinitely more beautiful and fruitful, and I hope to convince my readers of this. I would like to help them to make friends, to deepen their friendships and to find more creative joy in them.

We shall first consider the lonely man, the sad lot of he who has no friends. Sometimes sociological conditions make it impossible or highly difficult for certain persons to make friends. Sometimes, and probably more frequently, the obstacles are rather psychological, within the subject himself. We shall analyze the specific characteristics of friendship between men, between women, between men and women, between husband and wife, between parents and children and also between teachers and students. Then we shall try to give a satisfactory answer to a much-debated question: can we sustain several friendships or must we restrict ourselves to one? We shall compare the two most intense emotional experiences, friendship and love, but we will be careful not to set up artificial conflicts between them. After distinguishing the specific nature of friendship from other interpersonal relationships, such as solidarity and companionship, we shall analyze the primordial role of friendship in promoting authentic existence. At the same time we shall call attention to the obstacles which threaten it and the means we must use to overcome them. Our most ardent desire is that this book will contribute in some small way to promoting a social order in which the bonds of friendship will prevail over antagonisms and self-interest.

I

The solitude
and uprootedness
of modern man

"MAN is born and dies alone and it is only by deluding himself, between these two cardinal events, that he can believe that he is not alone." So say the spokesmen of pessimism, of whom Jean Paul Sartre is probably the most eloquent representative today. Can such pessimism be supported by arguments from concrete experience? Not entirely, in our opinion. Many children come into the world surrounded by tenderness and love which remains profoundly imprinted on their souls and protects them from feeling abandoned all their life, despite the disappointing experiences they encounter. Too, I have seen dying people who seem to maintain the most intense communion with those they love until their last breath. And since we are speaking as a psychologist and not as a metaphysician, to maintain that the question we have to do with here is one of illusory behavior or bad faith means absolutely nothing.

Having said this, we must note that it is the lot of many men and women to live in total solitude, not only at the moments of their birth and death but throughout life. This is probably more true in our own age than ever before, both because of the sociological uprootedness of many of our contemporaries and because of a more intense awareness of selfhood. When most men are more conscious of their appurtenance to a social group than of their individuality they do not feel abandoned unless some misfortune separates them from the social group of which they are a part, and this, after all, happens rarely enough. In the present state of the development of self-awareness, a phenomenon frequently appears which at first sight seems very paradoxical: namely, solitude is never greater or more painful than in our large cities. There people live in huge complexes or in hotel rooms where the least noise is heard by the neighbors, where often the least intimacy is made difficult. In the congested streets and subways we are constantly jostled. Many complain that they can never be alone, that they can never find the opportunity for the minimal reflection necessary for a balanced life. What is worse, many men and women today have become, by force of habit, psychically incapable of being alone and, therefore, of recollecting themselves, of becoming aware of their true situation in the world. They feel an imperious need to go to the cinema or to bars or to go dancing—not because they particularly want to see a film, have a drink or dance, but simply because life outside the crowd is intolerable for them. During vacations they "absolutely must" go where everyone else goes.

It seems, then, that man was never less alone than in our times, and if he has a complaint, it should be about his lack of solitude rather than the presence of it. In reality, the paradox is a superficial one. There is no contradiction between psychological solitude and the physical absence of solitude. Nowhere, in fact, is man more totally and more painfully alone than in a crowd. Hermits in the desert are infinitely less alone than the inhabitants of our large cities who are constantly thrown together. Not to confuse the physical isolation of the hermit with the moral solitude of the city dweller we shall call the latter phenomenon *loneliness*. To overcome loneliness it is not enough to break out of our physical isolation by becoming absorbed in an anonymous crowd. What is tragic about the condition of modern man, and what constitutes his loneliness, is the absence of dialogue, of spiritual communication with others. The hermit in the desert can communicate with God, with those dear to him by prayer and reflection, and with all of mankind if his capacity for love has attained such universal dimensions. The lonely one neither converses nor communicates with anyone. More seriously, he is frequently radically incapable of real existential communication—so much so that, consciously at least, he feels no need of such communication.

I have often had occasion in my work to encourage men living in complete loneliness to seek communication with others because this seemed to me the only way of protecting them from the gravest psychic illness. More often than not they have refused, protesting that they were terrified of others, that they were never more at ease than when they were alone. Yet, each time I had the opportunity of knowing such lovers of solitude better, it became clear that unconsciously they suffered from their loneliness; their unhappiness and their pessimistic vision of human nature was conditioned by it. Unconsciously almost all of those who sought escape in the theaters, dance halls, bars and other public places were seeking emotional communication with others. And the self-styled misanthropes who locked themselves in their apartments with their cats and canaries bore unconscious ill will toward others for not having accepted them.

The crowd we meet in public places, far from favoring dialogue and communication, in reality makes them difficult—if not impossible. Relationships formed in such circumstances are fatally superficial and impersonal; they are purely functional. How could it be otherwise since almost all who gather in such places live in a state of unauthenticity; they have not become aware of who they are themselves, of who others are or of what they are looking for in each other.

Many young people who have come to me confess their inability to bear solitude, even for a few hours. As a means of escape they join groups that meet on weekends; all of their leisure time is spent with the group. They are not delinquents, but boys and girls of good families, students at the university or in the best schools. They do not spend long hours in the cafés because they like strong drink (for the most part they drink soft drinks) or because they are addicted to card games and pinball machines. They gather simply to be together. I have made some effort to find out what they talk about. I have questioned them in detail and thus learned of the total emptiness of most of their conversations.

"How's it going?"

"Not bad. And you?"

Their working vocabulary is so extraordinarily impoverished that real communication is impossible. A film they have seen is described as "terrific" or a "dud." No effort is made to explain the reason for so summary a judgment. Their comments are habitually monosyllabic. They generally part with the sense of having wasted their time, disillusioned with one another for not having said anything worthwhile. But as they are incapable of any other kind of communication they hasten to meet again as soon as possible.

The majority of relationships between adults are no better. It is quite frightening to listen to conversations between educated people at a dinner or a cocktail party. In most cases they have little to say to one another. The success of certain games, such as bridge, can undoubtedly be explained in terms of the illusion they give people of escaping their solitude without the burden of conversation. But these palliatives cannot afford any solution to the agonizing problem posed by the loneliness of modern man.

The family itself is most frequently a mere juxtaposition of solitudes. Members think they know one another because they are always together, while in reality no one is truly open with anyone else. Of course, an illusion of love is maintained, but it is a purely instinctive, animal love in which the specifically human faculties play little part. There is no *understanding*, not even suspicion that there is something to understand in parents or children, in brothers or sisters. The majority of conjugal misunderstandings that I have encountered professionally were not due to sexual incompatibility but to an almost total lack of communication of minds. Sexual incompatibility itself, as we shall establish in a later chapter, is more frequently than not the result of a lack of spiritual communication. This lack is felt most acutely by those who are most intellectually developed.

In many cases this disparity between intellectual maturity and emotional poverty, the principal cause of the lack of communication, gives rise to more or less serious neuroses. Michael, fifty-five years old and very depressed, has no taste for life and views everything in a pessimistic light. The judgment he passes on people in general and on his friends in particular is altogether cynical. He has attempted suicide several times and blames cowardice for his not daring to go all the way. Yet he has a high-paying and socially flattering position. He is married to a fine woman who takes good care of him and with whom he has few difficulties. His children do well in their studies and otherwise give him no trouble. Why, then, his "complex of unhappiness," his distaste for life?

In the course of analysis it became clear that Michael had never experienced a genuine emotional contact in his life. He is "good," everyone treats him well; but no one ever really has loved him any more than he has ever loved anyone. He contracted a conventional marriage. His relationship to his children is based on "principles." He does his duty by them, they obey him, but there is no spirit on either side. Michael is thus painfully aware that neither his wife nor children, neither his colleagues nor friends understand him. Later in analysis he admitted that he never made any effort to understand others, nor to make his real self known to them. Moreover, until he gained some insight from analysis (his neurasthenia originally led him to consult a doctor) it never occurred to him that interpersonal relationships could or should go beyond get-

ting along together. For a long time he was perfectly satisfied with his lot. When he later became haunted by feelings of failure and unhappiness he saw no link between his
illness and what he called his "unsociability." During
treatment he learned to conduct a dialogue first of all with
his analyst, then with his family and finally with his colleagues at work. Friendships were born and his whole life
was transformed, as well as his conception of the world
and humanity.

The existence and the nefarious character of the extraordinary loneliness in modern man seems incontestable.
We must now ask: Is this situation irreversible and irremediable or is there some solution? Psychotherapy, after
all, is of limited value when the condition is in its advanced
stages. We know the answer that Sartre gives: Anyone
who has seen beyond the banalities of daily life and has
come to some knowledge of himself (Sartre's "for itself")
can only see himself as alone and lonely. Self-awareness is
synonymous with unhappiness precisely because we then
realize the radical impossibility of effecting that communion with others which everyone believes to be the
sine qua non condition of their happiness. Love, friendship and camaraderie are likewise the result of the unconscious bad faith of men who are too cowardly to admit
their irremediable solitude. From *L'Être et le Néant* to
Le Diable et le bon Dieu to *Les Chemins de la Liberté* and
Huis-Clos, all of Sartre's work has had as one of its essential themes man's inability, connatural to the human
condition itself, of breaking out of his intolerable solitude
by means of encounter with others. The "other" is necessarily the enemy for Sartre.

We would not accord such importance to Sartre's pessimism were it only a question of a literary technique or a personal neurosis on the part of the philosopher. But his influence upon so many novelists who have popularized his ideas and upon so many young people is because his own existential experience coincides at least partially with that of many of his contemporaries. He is a spokesman for an important part of mankind today.

But a philosophy of fatal loneliness and consequent unhappiness cannot claim to express the totality of human experience. In terms of our personal experience, both direct and indirect, we must protest the pessimism of Sartrian existentialism, at least in so far as it pretends to render an adequate account of the whole human condition. Encounter with another, by virtue of his otherness, is as a matter of fact the central event in the life of most men. We have observed that such encounters, far from being merely a cause of illusions and deceptions, in most cases afford men an excellent opportunity of realizing themselves and fulfilling their vocation as men. If this is unfortunately not always the case, if, particularly in our time, encounter with another rarely matures into authentic communication, the explanation must be sought not in some existential impossibility but more simply in the conditions of the psychosociological life of modern man, in the disharmony between his intellectual and emotional development.

Genuine communication with others can take very different forms, but it is always and necessarily of the emotional order. In a uniquely intellectual exchange each puts forth his ideas and thoughts, but not his very being. Communication remains extrinsic probably because certain philosophers and their disciples know only a kind of interminable discussion—on politics, literature and art, whether in a meeting hall or in a café, and they believe they have a duty to affirm the impossibility of man's breaking out of his loneliness. Because the human person is capable of escaping his solitude and of being loved, loneliness is not a necessary characteristic of the human condition.

Emotional energy, what we may call "libido" in the Jungian sense, is clearly not at the disposition of all men in the same quantity or in the same quality. Some are emotionally rich while others are extremely poor, just as some are more and some are less gifted intellectually. As a result of neurotic conflicts emotional energy can be greatly inhibited or repressed even in those who initially were superiorly endowed with it—so much so that in some cases we can rightly speak of a veritable emotional atrophy. Moreover, superior emotional wealth does not always go hand in hand with intellectual superiority. Some men have great intellectual gifts but are astonishingly deprived emotionally, just as the opposite may be the case.

Theresa, a young university student, went to see a psychotherapist because she felt herself incapable of love. She experienced none of the strong passions usually associated with love with her lovers, her parents or her friends. In the course of treatment I learned that Theresa was very highly egocentric, although she was not an egoist. But her egocentricity was a compensation for her inferiority complex, her lack of confidence in herself. (For, contrary to popular opinion, egocentricity, far from being an excess of self-love, is rather a lack or an absence of it.) When analysis liberated her from her inferiority complex by giving her normal self-confidence, her emotional relations with others soon became normal. This marked the end of her loneliness.

In several of my earlier books I criticized Freud and his followers for considering emotional energy, the libido, as specifically sexual in nature. In this hypothesis the only really authentic form of communication between people would be sexual love. All other attachments and affections, in such a hypothesis, would be the result of deviations, repressions or sublimations of the sexual libido. Jung has a much truer view of the matter. Emotional energy is essentially undifferentiated. An individual can make different uses of the quantity and the quality of emotional energy at his disposal. At least theoretically, one who expends emotional energy intensively in sexual love will have little left for creative activities, for the service of the community or for the love of God. In practice, however, this is not always the case. Frequently a man's passionate love for a woman increases his capacity to love God, his parents or friends—all renewing his creative élan. On the other hand, we have had occasion to note in a number of cases that when a man achieves an authentic love for God or mankind his capacity for erotic love increases proportionately. In therapy we have had success in curing those who were impotent or frigid by awakening in them a powerful interest in a meaningful cause. But an abuse of emotional energy in a given domain has harmful consequences for the totality of emotional life. Libertinism considerably inhibits creativity and relationships to the human community and to God. Bigotry, which is to the love of God what libertinism is to erotic love, renders the subject inept for the love of man as well as for all truly creative work. The same is true of that deviation of the love for creative work which is called *activism*. The libertine does not truly love erotically any more than the bigot truly loves God or the activist truly loves creative activity. All remain imprisoned in their solipsism and are thus incapable of reaching true emotional communication.

Some years ago I devoted a long study to an analysis of erotic love (*The Psychology of Loving*), considering its grandeur and misery, its chances of success and its risks of deviation. Experience shows that erotic love cannot fully satisfy the need for existential communion that all men more or less obscurely desire. Not everyone can find a partner who is erotically adequate and with whom he can achieve authentic interpersonal communion. Quite often the "perfect" sexual partners remain isolated in their solitude. Too, there are vocations or conditions of life that are incompatible with erotic communion. Moreover, there are times in the lives of everyone that are not conducive to erotic union, such as adolescence and old age. Finally, even those whose erotic love life is nearly perfect do not find it fully satisfying, for it is at best a highly fragile possession. In order to endure, it must be allied to other forms of emotional life that are less dependent upon the mutations of the flesh.

The most universal and, in our opinion, the noblest of all forms of interhuman communication, the only one capable of dissolving our loneliness, is friendship. He who has no friends can only have a very pessimistic view of life and the human condition, whatever joy he may otherwise derive from life. A true friendship, on the contrary, guarantees happiness and even joy in the midst of the worst tribulations. According to whether or not one believes in the possibility of authentic friendship, one will see in loneliness either an unhappy accident or, instead, the fate of the human condition. These are not the conclusions of abstract reasoning but of concrete experience.

II

The birth of
friendship

It seems clear that friendship can be established at all levels of the human condition. Already, in groups of children, we observe that preferred relationships spring up between little ones four or five years old although they may have been strangers a few days before. It frequently happens that two children whose parents live in the same building and who have known each other all their lives make different friends at school. This is often true of brothers and sisters. The friends parents choose for their children rarely suit the latter and not infrequently the friends they choose themselves do not please their parents, although we cannot affirm a priori that it is always because of an emotional reaction on the part of children who are jealous of their independence and resent parental encroachment.

Deep friendships exist among criminals as well as among geniuses and saints. A writer who spent some time in a mental hospital relates in a novel how strong bonds of friendship united two of his unfortunate companions. They conducted themselves as friends not only in their moments of lucidity but also when they were under the spell of delirium. In this state both lost sense of reality, one taking himself to be a horse, the other a dog. They trotted about on all fours, acting out their respective fantasies. Even so, they remained very fond of one another and each seemed to understand the other admirably. Their friendship alone seemed to resist the destructive tendency of madness. We ourselves have observed the existence of selective friendships in an institution for abnormal children whose sensibilities were as yet very embryonic.

André Malraux, in *Les Noyers de l'Altenburg*, shows that friendship can exist even between two enemy soldiers. This was also Romain Rolland's thesis in his celebrated *Jean-Christophe*. Friendship is not arrested either by national boundaries or by class barriers. When I was young I was well acquainted with two boys who were inseparable friends. Later, under the German occupation, one dedicated himself to the resistance movement and became a communist. The other, apparently in equally good faith, was an active combatant in a Fascist party whose sympathies were with Nazi Europe. There is no reason to suppose that either would have betrayed his cause in order to save the other. And yet, to the great scandal of their respective comrades, they continued to consider themselves good friends. When they chanced to meet, it sufficed that the conversation turn on something other than politics to bring the emotional current of their friendship alive again. Similar bonds of friendship likewise exist between men of different religions, indeed, between believers and atheists. In such cases, it is always true that the men involved have attained a relatively superior degree of psychic maturity and are for this reason better able to understand those who do not share their faith and their convictions.

Among the less mature, as we shall see later, friendship presupposes a likeness of living conditions and an identity of opinion and belief.

Those who are most spiritually advanced and most detached from worldly things generally do not scorn friendship. We know from the Gospel of Jesus' affection for his disciple John, the son of Zebedee, as well as for Lazarus and his sister. Since it pleased Him to take on the human condition, The Son of God Himself did not disdain the joys of friendship. This is also true of most of those who imitated Him best, the saints and ascetics. It is significant that many among them believed they had to break all human ties and even despise all the goods of this world, yet they never believed themselves obliged to renounce friendship. St. Anthony, who is taken to be the most austere of the desert Fathers and whose ascetic practices strike us as excessive, left the desert only because of friendship. His friend Athanasius, bishop of Alexandria, was suffering persecution and Anthony hastened to lend him assistance. Even in monasteries of strict observance, where the rule forbids particular friendship, friendships are born and flourish.

However, it is true that errors in the teaching on asceticism and detachment lead many religious men to believe it a duty to fight inclinations toward "particular" friendships (as though there could be a friendship that was not particular!) and to accuse themselves of it as a fault in confession or before the community. I do not believe that such a repression of one of the noblest, if not the noblest, sentiments of the human heart can favor spiritual progress. But that is another question about which we shall have more to say later.

The evidence seems clear: friendship is the most universal of all interhuman relations in the emotional order. The simple and the advanced, criminals and saints taste its joys and find in it the means of overcoming their loneliness. The question we must now ask is upon what basis is friendship established between two people. We have seen that friendship has its source in emotional energy, in the libido. The more that people are quantitatively and qualitatively rich in libido, the more are their friendships strong and rich. There is an immense qualitative difference between the friendship that united Socrates and his disciples and that which binds a gang of hooligans. But we are not raising that question for the moment; rather: why does our libido turn toward one person rather than toward another? According to what conscious or unconscious criteria do we choose our friends, supposing that we do truly choose them?

We have noted earlier that friendship can be born between men of very different religions, countries and professions. Nonetheless, all friendship implies a certain degree of communion; a certain likeness must exist between friends, a more or less essential community of interests. An artist generally chooses his friends from among other artists, a scholar from among scholars, a Communist from among Communists, and so forth. Of course, a Communist painter could be the friend of a Catholic painter, and I know of deep friendships between Christians and Moslems. In the first case, the love of painting creates a communion sufficiently strong to resist the ideological divergences, and the second case involves those who have transcended the sociohistorical stage of religious faith. Their psychic maturity is adequate to enable them to understand and love those who think and feel differently than they do, to discern what they have in common, not in spite of, but beyond differences. In the case of those who are psychologically less mature, the birth of friendship presupposes a more tangible likeness of living conditions as well as a greater identity of opinions and beliefs.

A community of interests, whether these be "sublime" or terrestrial, is not in itself enough to account for the birth of friendship between two human beings. Let us take a young man who belongs to a musical club, all of whose members profess the same political and religious convictions as himself. If, after some time, he becomes friends with another young man from another group, it is not necessarily because their ideological or musical company is more perfect, nor is it even because they mutually recognize one another as "better." It is a matter of ordinary experience that we do not always choose as a friend he who, objectively or subjectively, seems to be better than our other acquaintances. Even the sublime friendship of predilection that Christ showed to His disciple John in no way proves that He thought him better than the other disciples. It was, after all, to Peter that He confided the government of His Church. Just as a lover might well recognize that some other woman is more beautiful than the one who is the object of his passion, I may well admit, without the least harm to him, that my friend is neither the most intelligent nor the most generous of my acquaintances, any one of whom could probably also become my friend. In any case, the young musician we have spoken of admits that there are better musicians than his friend in his group and even that he can converse more easily with others than with his rather taciturn friend. Yet he chooses him as his friend.

However important be the qualities of the other, they

are certainly not adequate to explain why we choose precisely this one for a friend. There are also friendships that transpire like a bolt from the blue, psychologically similar to certain kinds of love. We meet so and so for the first time; we know little about him; we scarcely know what he thinks or what his tastes are; but we immediately become very sympathetic toward him; we more or less consciously want to attract his attention and awaken in him a similar sympathy toward us. This kind of sudden attraction is not yet friendship to be sure; it is merely a first spark and numerous conditions are necessary to give rise to a true flame of friendship, one capable of resisting the vicissitudes of life. Nonetheless, the simple fact that such a spark arises indicates that the birth of friendship originates to a large extent in unconscious motives, as is the case, for that matter, in almost all our other emotional activities.

However many rational motives we are able to adduce as reasons for loving someone, they cannot furnish an adequate account. This does not mean that sudden friendships take place without motives, for these are far from always being exclusively rational. Our consciousness may be still ignorant of the other, yet our unconscious may already have recognized him as a possible friend, have divined between him and us mysterious affinities that will perhaps take years to become fully conscious. The unconscious seems to divine sometimes not only what the other already is, but further, what he is capable of becoming, perhaps precisely because of our friendship. It divines between the other and ourselves a potential kinship of souls. It is important, too, to recognize that unconscious motives, like conscious ones, are far from being wholly egoistical. What we have the right to expect and receive from the other is important, but equally important is what we think we are more or less capable of giving him. Friendship is essentially *generous*.

If friendship is to transpire between two people, it is important that both be in a state of *availability*. I have often been in the company of those who complain that they have no friends. Inevitably, I have observed that this condition was due to their own lack of availability; they were too encumbered to be able to welcome another. Such unavailability may be exterior in nature; that is, people may lack the time or the emotional energy necessary for friendship. This is particularly the case with many businessmen who are obliged by their profession to have innumerable contacts and social encounters. They talk of everything except what is truly personal to each one. Very seldom can a true friendship blossom under such conditions.

But the most frequent kind of unavailability is of an interior, subjective nature. The other, as "other," does not interest the egoist. He would like to have a friend, but only for the egotistical satisfactions that the other might provide. The narcissist sees in another a kind of mirror of his own hypertrophic self. Any dissimilarity or divergence seems to him to be an insurmountable obstacle to what he understands by friendship. He tolerates no contradiction, expects the other to listen to him and approve of him and be always ready to receive him. If he feels the need, he will visit the other daily without respect for his personal life or other friends. Then he may not appear for days or weeks simply because he has no desire to. It little matters to him that the other may be lonely. Naturally enough such a "friend" is disappointing and is instinctively avoided. Sometimes egocentric unavailability is the result of a neurosis, and only a good psychotherapist can help make the subject capable of friendship. In other cases a certain awareness and voluntary effort suffice.

There are degrees of availability and therefore greater or lesser chances for friendships to exist. If friendship blossoms more often and more easily in youth than in adulthood or old age, it is because young persons are generally more available. Consequently many men and women have only those friends they made when they were young. If these should disappear, they would feel incapable of making new friends. I know an old woman over eighty who is always ready to make a new friend and she does so among those of her own generation as well as among young people. One might say that such a person has remained young at heart. Nonetheless, normally, the mature adult who is not neurotic ought to be more fitted for friendship than the adolescent, provided he has succeeded in protecting his personal life at least partially from the distractions of the world. A certain degree of narcissism is, after all, normal with adolescents, and if they nonetheless do succeed in making friends, it is because their availability is greater than their narcissistic tendencies. The need and the desire for friendship triumphs over the fear of love. But, unless he is inhibited by psychic conflicts, the adult ought to be more immune to the temptation to narcissism. And the exterior obstacles to availability ought to be more easily conquered, on the condition, of course, that his desire for friendship is not a mere impulse.

The desire for friendship, we have seen, often springs from the emotional depths of our psyche well before we have acquired a rational knowledge of the other person. Our libido is stimulated by our disposition toward friendship, by our need for friendship. But if our desire carries us toward a particular person rather than toward others, it is because our subconscious recognizes in him a potential partner in dialogue and communion. It has divined instinctively something in common, some fundamental kinship between the other and ourselves; otherwise, dialogue would be unthinkable. Real dialogue, on the other hand, cannot take place between those who are so much alike that one is a mere echo of the other. Differences and complementary differences are at least as important as likenesses if friendly communion is to become possible. Moreover, in order to estimate the viability of a friendship between ourselves and another, our unconscious takes inventory not so much of the static self as of the ideal self.

Many factors enter into the formation of our ideal of the self, of that ideal image that we would like to realize in ourselves and which gives a certain unity to our energies and our scattered efforts. The child's ideal of self is made up almost entirely of the projected image he has unconsciously formed of his parents, although it is not necessarily an exact portrait of them. The girl wants to become like her mother and the boy wants to resemble his father. Frequently the child is in emotional conflict with one or the other of his parents, especially because he believes himself to be little or badly loved by them. Then his ideal of the self is the exact opposite of the parent with whom he is in conflict; he wishes to become radically different from the latter. Thus the child chooses his friends not in function of what he is himself, but in function of the ideal of self he has formed from his parents. A small boy who at home is loved in an overly protected manner by his mother may at school seek out a friend who is stronger and more popular, someone who can play the same role of protector toward him. It is also possible that he unconsciously rebels against this excessive maternal protection, even though he may consciously be very much at ease with it. Then, by a process of psychological compensation, he will become attached to someone who is weaker and whom he can protect and dominate.

Little by little, beginning with adolescence, the ideal of self becomes more complex and is nourished by sources other than the family. The heroes of novels and films, historical personalities, admired teachers all contribute in different degrees to the formation of our ideal of self. Most frequently all of this takes place in a confused manner, but in spite of that influences no less the number of our decisions and choices, in particular the choice of our friends.

We want to realize this ideal of self in our own persons and more or less assiduously strive to do so. But we seek it primarily in those whom we wish to make our friends. Each time the desire for friendship with a particular person we have met for the first time arises in us, it is because our unconscious has already divined that at least in some respects his personality corresponds to our ideal of the self, either actually or potentially.

But it is not enough for the birth of friendship that the other more or less conform to our ideal of the self. It is also necessary that our ideal of self coincide at least partially with his ideal of self. The lack of such a coincidence often smothers our impulse to friendship.

Erotic love often enough is only unilateral. This is usually the case with adolescents who do not dare ask for reciprocity from the object of their desire. With adults unrequited love was quite fashionable in the romantic era. However, it is rare that a bolt from the blue strikes two people at the same moment. At least for a time most loves are unrequited. "Does it matter if I love you?" a romantic lover asks his loved one. Literature and life are equally rich in examples of unrequited love. Most frequently, when this state of things is prolonged, we have what is conventionally called an "unhappy love." But I also know of cases where the lover whose love is unrequited accepts non-reciprocity without too much suffering and finds in his very love the source of great existential enrichment. Thus Max, a young man who had fallen very low morally, fell in love with the wife of his best friend. Knowing this woman to be virtuous and in love with her husband, Max had no hope of winning her love and, in fact, did nothing to bring it about. But at least he wanted to become worthy of the woman he loved, and this effort brought about a radical conversion in his way of life.

Friendship, on the contrary, is inconceivable without reciprocity. Of course we can speak of being a friend of nature or a friend of animals without entailing the idea of reciprocity. But this is a purely analogical extension of the word friendship. In its proper meaning, friendship always and necessarily implies dialogue and communion and thus supposes, by definition, two terms. I cannot call myself the friend of so and so without being certain that he too is disposed to recognize me as his friend.

The demand for reciprocity obviously makes the birth of friendship more risky. I might well believe that a certain person is the perfect incarnation of my ideal of self and feel a powerful impulse of friendship toward him, but if he does not recognize in me his own ideal of self, or more simply, if he is not for the moment disposed toward friendship, my impulse will very likely meet with no welcome. The temptation is then great, and many succumb to it, to believe that friendship is impossible, to judge oneself unworthy of the friendship of those one would like to have for friends. It is, however, pure romanticism to believe that our ideal of self can only be realized in one person, and that, if he does not desire us as a friend, we are therefore definitively condemned to loneliness. It is first of all necessary to realize that no one human being can perfectly realize our ideal of self and, secondly, that there are several, perhaps many, who reflect it partially, in different degrees, but sufficiently for authentic existential communion to take place between us and each one of them. He who seeks friendship with sincerity and perseverance has every chance of finding it one day. What is important is never to be discouraged by failures, however repeated they may be.

The situation of one whose friendship is solicited is not always any more comfortable than that of one who is in search of friendship. Personally, I have experienced the embarrassments of this predicament many times. Mr. X is an assiduous reader of my books; he thinks he has found in them the solution to his personal problems. He is under the impression that no one better than the author of these books is able to understand him and therefore be his friend. He writes to me, comes to see me, invites me to his home and soon offers me his friendship. What should I do? I pity him, am sympathetic toward him and am altogether willing to understand and help him. But he expects something more from me. Yet it is clear from the beginning that I expect nothing from him and, therefore, no reciprocity, no true friendship is possible between us.

The same situation repeats itself from time to time with those who come to me for treatment. Most frequently there is no question of "transference" in the strict Freudian sense of the term, that is to say, of a shifting of the neurotic conflict upon the therapist. More simply, in the course of therapeutic sessions the patients become more acutely aware of their loneliness and the alienation that results from it. A strong desire for communication with another is born in them and to the degree that their neurotic inhibitions fall away, they feel more and more disposed toward friendship. What is more natural than to desire and to believe in the possibility of a true and deep friendship precisely with the one in whom they have confided and who seems to understand them so well? For many, the psychotherapist is the first person to have taken them seriously, to have listened attentively to them and to have shown them sympathy. They are therefore easily inclined to think that he is the only one who can do this and therefore the only possible friend. There are cases where a true relationship of friendship can take place between a psychotherapist and his patient, a friendship that will last long after the therapy has terminated and without any possibility of countertransference.

In most cases, however, the patient knows very well, and does not have to be told, that he cannot count on any real reciprocity from the therapist. This is a cause of some suffering; he regrets having nothing to give in return for what he has received. The psychologist must tactfully encourage him to dispose himself to friendships that are available within the normal environment of his life. The therapist can make the patient understand that if previously he had not met any friends this was because of his neurotic conflicts, obstacles which no longer ought to exist. And he will get the patient's free consent for the very particular kind of emotional relationships that can and, indeed, must exist during psychological treatment, relationships which are neither erotic nor, properly speaking, friendship. I have often noticed that this *sui generis* emotional relationship with the psychotherapist serves the patient as an apprenticeship to friendship. Many establish solid friendships before their treatment is completed with persons whom they sometimes had known for years without having dared to hope that a friendship was possible between them. It is quite true that the chief problem, often the only obstacle to the birth of friendship, exists in the subject himself who complains of not having any friends.

Friendship must be willed. But more than this is necessary. Again, personal experience confirms this observation. A few years ago I worked on the same project with a man close to me in age and cultural interests. I had high respect for both his intelligence and his emotional qualities. We also found ourselves in perfect accord on ideological and spiritual matters. I have rarely so intensely desired to become anyone's friend; I confided my desire to him and from all evidence he had an identical desire. We made meritorious efforts to meet one another, endeavored to achieve as intimate a dialogue as possible and acted in all things like friends. It was all in vain; the emotional spark was not forthcoming. We had to resign ourselves to being good companions, "friends" in the broad sense of the term. We got along marvelously on the intellectual plane, but our emotional accord left something to be desired. Let those who have had a similar experience not infer the impossibility of friendship as such but only its impossibility with a given person.

Is the contrary also true? Can one become friends with someone without willing it? It seems not. True, we have spoken earlier of friendships that strike like a bolt from the blue, but this does not mature into true friendship until confirmed by the persons involved. We are never someone's friend despite ourselves. However obscure its origin, friendship can only develop in the full light of consciousness.

If friendship is to take root and flower, certain similarities—but also certain dissimilarities, as we have seen—are necessary. It seems clear that friendship is almost impossible between certain kinds of characters and temperaments. A man whom characterologists classify as active–primary–emotional would doubtless try in vain to establish a friendship with a nonactive–secondary–nonemotional type. There would have to be some similarity on at least one of these levels. Likewise, friendship is impossible between introverts and extroverts. Yet a certain extraversion is possible among the former, at least with the help of psychotherapy, just as a certain introversion can be effected among the latter. In this case they can form an ideal friendship, playing toward one another approximately the role which Jung attributed to the *anima* and the *animus*, and vice versa. Too great an identity of character or temperament often proves to be an obstacle to friendly communion. A friendship which encounters no difficulty risks remaining too superficial between two extroverts and too inefficaciously sentimental between two introverts.

Frequently enough we observe friendship between two

persons who appear to be radically different from one another. A pretty girl may have as a close friend a plain Jane or a good student may be inseparable from the worst dunce. Those involved are often the last to be able to give a satisfactory, rational explanation for such friendships. But it is not always true, as popular opinion affirms, that the pretty girl more or less consciously wants to show off her beauty by contrast with her ugly companion. Analysis frequently shows that it is often a case of a kind of compensation. The pretty girl or the good student has a more or less strong feeling of not deserving to be what they are, and their choice of friends is a kind of "payment." But it is also possible that the pretty girl or the strong student has unconsciously divined in the plain Jane and the dunce secret qualities which they themselves lack. A similar compensation may motivate the plain Jane and the dunce. In any case, nothing authorizes us to consider such friendships a priori unauthentic. Neurotic compensations certainly exist; but so do perfectly healthy compensations.

III

What friendship
is not

To properly understand the special reality of friendship, we must distinguish it from other interhuman relationships which may in some respect resemble it. Like many other words, the term "friendship" is often terribly misused in our day. We say or write "my dear friend" to people whom we scarcely know. Often we say it with a certain note of condescension. A given employer readily calls his subordinates "dear friends" but would scarcely permit them to address him in the same fashion. It is common to say: "he is one of my friends" when we are speaking of someone we meet socially from time to time.

As a result of this exaggerated extension of the concept of friendship many no longer realize that true friendship can exist, the kind of friendship we are speaking of in this book, which can play a decisive role in the promotion of life. They, therefore, do nothing to dispose themselves to such friendship and thus renounce the only chance they have of escaping the loneliness from which they suffer.

It is in no sense our intention to idealize unduly the

notion of friendship. As we said in the first chapter, friendship is not a rare privilege. To some degree it embellishes the life of saints and sinners, of adults and children, of scholars and the ignorant. But it does not follow that we are entitled to call any interhuman relation "friendship." By clearly distinguishing what friendship is from what it is not, our intention is not thereby to discredit other forms of interhuman relations. Most of them play an important and positive role in the individual and collective life of human beings. But these relationships are something other than friendship, and the role that falls to them is different from that of friendship.

Human solidarity is the basis of all interhuman communication. In former ages the awareness of this solidarity was quite precisely limited. One felt solidarity with a family, a tribe, a nation and, later, with a class. It was difficult to imagine that one could be friends with anyone other than those of the same group. The prodigious development of the means of travel and communication is gradually doing away with these boundaries. More and more numerous are those who spontaneously think of themselves as members of the human race before they are aware of national, racial, class or religious solidarity. Such men and women in no way think they have done their whole duty by acquitting themselves of their obligations toward their family or their native country. Famine in China, slavery in Arabia, racism in South Africa, the persecution of Protestants in Spain and of Christians generally in Communist countries concern them personally. They feel in some way responsible for all of these evils and think it their duty to do what they can to fight them. With some the awareness of solidarity goes beyond the human com-

munity and takes on properly cosmic proportions. Following the example of St. Francis, they consider themselves
friends of the beasts and the flowers, of the whole universe.

It is true that the awareness of universal solidarity is
not absolutely new. Not only did the saints like Francis
of Assisi and so many others experience it to a very high
degree, but so too did the Stoics and other philosophers of
Greece and Rome, of the Renaissance, of the East and the
West. In such cases, however, relatively few individuals
were involved, the minority whose spiritual evolution was
far ahead of the majority of their contemporaries and
compatriots. What is specifically new in our age is the
unprecedented extension of the awareness of universal
solidarity. It is not yet ideally realized; indeed, from time
to time we witness tumultuous relapses into national or
racial fanaticism. But such failures are nonetheless relapses
of the spiritual élan which we have analyzed in several of
our earlier books. The evolution of the noosphere is undoubtedly irreversible and, because of that fact, the awareness of universal solidarity can only become greater.

It follows that interhuman relations, whether they be of
the economic, intellectual or emotional order, will be less and
less constricted by limitations. Friendships are already common between men who formerly would have considered it a
duty to fight and hate one another. But it is all the more
necessary to distinguish friendship from what it is not, for
the confusion can only harm both friendship and other
interhuman relations.

The young today easily confuse an intimate friend with
a casual companion. Yet the two are very different. Casual
companions are members of the same set, which resembles
less a community of persons than a flock whose awareness

is principally gregarious. Such companions go out together and frequent the same place of distraction, but make little effort to know each other intimately, more personally. I have frequently talked to young people about their relations with their companions. Most often they are ignorant of their companions' families, their studies, their professional activities, their projects for the future. Their encounters are almost always limited to banalities. Generally, they have become companions by pure chance, having met at a dance hall, a surprise party or on the beach. All these young people have in common is a predilection for the twist or some other fashionable dance or they are all "fanatics" for the same current singer. Such companions are, moreover, much more at ease in a group than in pairs, for in the first case they have only to shout and laugh together, while in pairs they would have to say something to one another—and they have nothing to say. Feelings of love and friendship can spring up between companions who then generally separate from the group and cease to be casual companions.

Mark is an interior decorating student, nineteen years old. He complained of being terribly bored because he felt so much alone. I learned that Mark belonged to a certain set, that he went to the theater and dancing with them several times a week and spent hours with them in popular cafés. Without being able to explain why he felt so alone while surrounded by so many companions (whom he sometimes called friends), he was nonetheless aware of the emotional inadequacy of this form of relationship. One day, after a holiday of some weeks, I found Mark a changed person. His gaiety was no longer artificial, he was no longer disgusted by life and no longer complained of being bored or alone. During his vacation Mark had made a "true" friend. He no longer has any desire to go out with his former companions, preferring to be with his friend. The great novelty of this relationship in his eyes is that he and his friend "understand one another" even when they pass hours together without saying anything. There is now no need to explain to this young man the difference between a friend and a casual companion; he knows that even the "best companion" is not the equivalent of a friend.

One of the most widespread interhuman relationships of our age results from sharing the same profession. Those who work together are evidently not friends, even though they may occasionally call themselves this in public, but colleagues. Generally, relations between colleagues are purely objective and do not in any way extend beyond the professional realm. Each profession has its banquets and annual conventions, but the resultant relationships are scarcely personal. The solidarity that may exist between colleagues most often exists with respect to a third person; with respect to each other they are rather competitors and usually conduct themselves as such. Moreover, those who work together on the same project and whose interests are truly solidary do not call themselves colleagues but rather comrades.

There is no doubt that camaraderie is existentially superior to either the relationships of casual companions or colleagues. Comrades are not content to amuse themselves together, nor is their relationship founded on the exercise of the same profession. Because they are engaged in a common fight for a cause which is dear to them they treat one another as comrades. Thus, there are comrades of war, of party or of union. A particular form of camaraderie existed in prison camps during the war. Prisoners were united less by the combat they had formerly waged in common than by the suffering they endured together. It is significant that the bonds of camaraderie born of the war or captivity sometimes survived the situation which gave birth to them by many years.

André Malraux, in several of his novels, has exalted the communion between war comrades. Men who fight side by side against the same enemy may well belong to different social, cultural, national, religious or political classes; the camaraderie of war abolishes all of these individual differences and makes all hearts beat in unison. Nothing seems more normal than to share one's last piece of bread, indeed, one's last poisonous pill with a comrade; one does not even hesitate to risk one's life to rescue a comrade from a dangerous situation. Because of camaraderie each one is capable of rising to a superior level of existence; camaraderie abolishes the banality of daily life.

For some ten years I had the opportunity of living personally, with much intensity, the mystique of camaraderie, and I am therefore in some position to testify that Malraux does not exaggerate its grandeurs. Our camaraderie was founded on our appurtenance to the same revolutionary party which we were aware of fighting for the "happy tomorrows," that is, for a future human society in which there would no longer be either inequalities of rights or wealth, or exploitation of man by man, or any other injustice. I remember a certain meeting in Moscow in the Red Square in which thousands of young people from all over the world participated. I have never experienced more strongly the deep meaning of camaraderie than when all together, each in his own language, we sang the *Interna-tional*. If the word "mystique" did not then have a pejora-tive sense for us, I would have spoken of a mystic com-munion among these young people. Between comrades the distinction between "mine" and "yours" no longer existed; it went without saying that each shared all. A fervent militant went so far as to offer his wife's companionship to a professional propagandist of the party whom he supposed to be long deprived of women because of his work.

From many points of view camaraderie can be mistaken for friendship. Yet it is not friendship. What is important in camaraderie is infinitely less the person of the comrade than his participation in a common struggle. It is true that bonds of particular affinity, of interpersonal predilection can be established, in which case we can say that comrades are also friends. But this friendship always remains sub-ordinate to the exigencies of combat and necessarily obeys the directives of the party.

Peter and John, whom I knew well, were both comrades and friends for a number of years. One day, the administra-tion of the party suspected Peter of entertaining relation-ships with the "enemies of the class," and it naturally charged John, his best friend, with spying upon him and eventually exposing him. If John had some hesitation or pain, he did not show it and found it normal to obey the party. The same thing took place in the great Stalinist purges, when Communists known for their courage re-nounced their best friends and, in a parody of justice, became witnesses against them. They certainly did not act out of cowardice. Even in free countries where one did not have much to fear from party headquarters those who at any given time felt obliged to break with the party lost all of their friends the moment they did so. From the Marxist point of view this can be perfectly justified. While friendship is a subjective relationship, camaraderie pertains to the objective order, and Marxism always subordinates the subjective to the objective. It is thus inconceivable, in this perspective, that one can remain friends when one has ceased to be a comrade. It follows that camaraderie itself, its beauties and grandeurs notwithstanding, constitutes a "closed" community in Bergson's sense of the word. There is certainly room for discussion as to whether or not this is superior to friendship; but it is clearly not the same thing as friendship and thus does not perform the same existential function as the latter.

IV

Friendship
and love

LOGICALLY, we ought to have analyzed the similarities and dissimilarities between friendship and love in the preceding chapter, following the comparisons of friendship to camaraderie and other interpersonal relationships. We devote a special chapter to it, however, because the connections between friendship and love are much more numerous and more intimate than those between friendship and camaraderie.

First, friendship and love are both subjective relationships. One loves a specific person or is his friend not because he belongs to the same nation, the same party or the same religion as oneself but, sometimes in spite of all that, simply because he is what he is. While it is easy to say why we consider a person our companion, colleague or comrade, it often proves much more difficult to give an account, to oneself as much as to others, of the motivations for our feelings of friendship and love. These motives are, as a matter of fact, often unconscious. Friendship and love are both emotional communications, while camaraderie

might well be very strong and authentic although the
comrades in question experience nothing genuinely heart-
felt toward one another. In seventeenth-century France
there was no distinction between the words "friend" and
"lover," so similar did friendship and love appear. Today,
however, it is important to become aware of both the
likenesses of and the differences between these two principal forms of emotional communion.

It would, no doubt, be idle to argue whether friendship
or love ought to occupy the first place among interpersonal
relationships. But it is uncontestable that both can bring
the individual out of his loneliness and enable him to live
a fuller life. One person may very legitimately argue that
friendship is more important in life, while another might
with as much reason uphold the contrary position. There
is often alternation of these two forms of emotional communion in the life of one person. Between children and
adolescents normally only bonds of friendship exist, and
with good reason we consider adolescence the age par
excellence for friendships. Young adults, generally without disdaining friendship, are inclined to give the first place
in their emotional life to love. It is, in effect, common for
a young man who has fallen in love with a young woman
to remove himself, at least for a time, from his friends,
although he may well take up with them some years later.
For adults, both friendship and love seem equally indispensable for the happiness and equilibrium of the person,
primacy sometimes given to one, at other times to the
other, depending upon the circumstances affecting the
individual. In maturity, especially among those who have
reached a superior spirituality, it is once again friendship
that becomes more important. As we shall have occasion

to note later, this alternation between friendship and love exists even in the life of married persons.

It is well known that the troubadours sang the beauties of a loving friendship. In reality they were referring to love, a love which in view of the morality and the mores of the age could only have been platonic. This kind of platonic love, which is very sincerely called friendship, is still common among adolescents who are only vaguely aware of the intimate bond that exists between their sexual impulses and their emotions. A loving friendship is certainly not impossible between adults, and under certain circumstances it can even be recommended. It is necessary, however, that the partners in question have solid moral and spiritual qualities if this friendship is not to become, despite their wishes, love as such. Illusions in this matter are only too easily born. But while it is true that love can disguise itself in certain cases as friendship, it would be a serious error to see in all friendship only disguised love. To be sure, the same emotional energy nourishes love and friendship, but as we have already said, this emotional energy, or libido, is in itself undifferentiated and takes its coloration from the feelings it feeds.

A certain degree of maturity, not only psychic but also physical, is necessary before one is capable of love. If the Freudians speak of a specifically sexual love in children, they do so by doctrinal assumption since according to them all affectivity, if not the totality of psychic life, is sexual in nature. In reality, a human being becomes capable of love only at the time of puberty. Of course, it is not necessary that love always tend consciously toward sexual union, and with adolescents this is generally not the case, but even the most platonic love is sexual in nature.

Physical maturity is in no way required for friendship. Although the superior and sublime kinds of friendship presuppose a high degree of psychic maturity, we are not thereby justified in considering as unauthentic friendships between children and adolescents, indeed, friendships between those who are even less mature. Friendship seems to be the most "natural" expression of human affectivity, which explains why it is found at all levels of emotional development. Moreover, friendship generally contributes most efficaciously to the emotional development of the individual. I have often noticed that those adults incapable of love are precisely those who have had no chance to apprentice to it in their childhood and adolescence by means of friendship.

Love, however sublime and sublimated we may suppose it to be, is necessarily a carnal passion. Consequently, it almost always implies certain difficulties, a certain clouding of one's intellectual and voluntary faculties. Even though love does not always take on the "demonic" qualities Dostoevski attributes to it, the literature of all peoples abounds with examples of love's crashing upon the subjects, despite themselves, like a bolt of lightning, like a stroke of fate. The wise men of antiquity, no less than more recent moralists, have warned their disciples against the passion of love, whose destructive tyranny they understood. It is undoubtedly for this same reason, more or less confusedly apprehended, that many religions, including Christianity, demand of their priests and other candidates for spiritual perfection the renunciation of carnal love. Rightly or wrongly (and in our opinion they are for the most part wrong), they believe it to be incompatible with an intense spiritual life.

However this may be, it is certain that the lover, insofar as he is under the influence of passion, has great difficulty in seeing his beloved with objectivity. Insofar as we love "passionately" we are conscious only of the excellent qualities of the other; much more, we even transform his or her most outstanding faults into virtues. A young girl of my acquaintance found her fiancé's stutter "marvelous," just as many men in love may, for example, find their beloved's squint charming. The matter becomes far more serious when love disguises as virtues the most scandalous moral deficiencies of the loved one. I knew a young girl of good family and excellent education and, additionally, of irreproachable personal morality, who loved a dissolute hoodlum; she saw feats of courage, almost the prowess of chivalry, in what in reality was no more than acts of burglary. But as soon as passion diminishes or disappears altogether, we often come to grips with the very real qualities of the other. How many husbands no longer in love with their wives see a form of mania in their love of neatness and order and yet at the same time regard their mistresses' slovenliness and disorder as admirable bohemianism! What appeared beautiful in the fire of passion suddenly seems so ugly!

I am not arguing that we ought to be indifferent to the physical qualities of our friends. We are very legitimately sensitive to their charm, beauty and strength and are justly proud of them. We are perhaps attracted to the melody of someone's voice or his gentle manner and thus a friendship begins. Nonetheless, the importance of the carnal element, in the broad sense we give the word here, is and remains secondary in the birth and development of friendship. Consequently, friendship is incomparably less subject to the eddies of sensibility than love. It is therefore much more serene. We accept our friends without illusion, with full knowledge of their virtues and faults. We are all evidently more indulgent toward the faults of our friends than toward those of people who are indifferent to us or, for much greater reason, antipathetic.

This is not, however, because friendship blinds us as love is said to do. On the contrary, the lucid affection we feel for our friends enables us to see more deeply, and thus we are in a better position to understand the exterior circumstances and the unconscious motives that might influence them and turn them from the path of righteousness. That very fine psychologist St. Augustine rightly says, "*Nemo nisi per amicitiam cognoscitur*"—we only know someone through friendship. Moreover, the clairvoyance in depth which friendship gives is not restricted to friends alone. Anyone who has had the experience of an authentic friendship and has therefore had the opportunity of penetrating the subjectivity of another will have acquired an experience that will be very beneficial to him in all his relations with others. Since we refuse to judge the behavior of our friends "objectively," that is, according to external appearances alone, we conclude with good logic that appearances convey only a very small part of the truth, even when it is not a question of our friends. Thus, we strive to know and to understand the changeable secrets of all those we encounter, even those who at first are antipathetic.

Paul, a twenty-eight-year-old student, was noted for the extreme severity, indeed, the malevolence, of his judgment concerning those about him. He saw egoism and stupidity everywhere and stated that "in our time" neither grandeur of soul, nor frankness and loyalty nor fidelity in love exist. Analysis showed that Paul had piteously failed in the few timid attempts he made to establish relationships of friendship and love, a failure owing to his own lack of availability. Several sessions of psychosynthesis sufficed to diminish, if not entirely liquidate, his narcissism, and the young man readily admitted, with a joy largely mixed with confusion, that he had at last become friends with a fellow student he had known for years but had not suspected as a potential friend. Little by little, thanks to this friendship, all of Paul's relations with those about him changed. He ceased judging summarily and severely his brothers and sisters as well as his comrades. If he spoke of someone's faults he immediately sought excusing causes. This comprehensive knowledge of others resulted in a very salutary appeasement of his tension, so much so that from the morose person he had been he became joyful and optimistic. Even on the political plane he gradually abandoned his former extremism.

Thus, friendship can be for us a veritable school of sympathy, susceptible of progressively extending itself to all human beings and finally to the cosmos itself.

Love is exclusive by nature; that is to say, it can only exist as reciprocity between two people. In effect, it implies as much carnal exchange as spiritual communion, and everyone knows that the flesh is attended by well-defined limits. Because of this fact, love is almost necessarily jealous. It is a universal experience, whether by intuition or by actual experience, that carnal attraction lacks stability. She who a short while ago appeared so beautiful may suddenly no longer attract our attention, not because she has changed but simply because our carnal libido has fixed itself upon another object. Psychologically there is nothing surprising about the feeling of insecurity that is inherent in love, even if the moral qualities of the other are in no way questioned, especially the other's sincerity. A woman may be absolutely sure of the authenticity of her husband's love and yet feel uneasy when she sees him become interested in another woman or speak of her enthusiastically. This explains, quite apart from any specifically religious perspective, why all societies tend to institutionalize love and surround it with the maximum of objective guarantees. In the early days of the Communist regime in Russia "free love" was preached, but the resultant insecurity was so catastrophic that the Soviet State was in danger of collapsing. It had no alternative but to resubject love to laws and regulations.

There is no place for jealousy in a friendship worthy of the name. As we shall analyze more closely, the friendship of a friend for other persons in no way affects the friendship that exists between him and me. On the contrary, we can only benefit from the enrichment which he acquires through other friendships. The domain of friendly communion is, in effect, of the spiritual order, and it is in the nature of the spirit not to know the limitations characteristic of the flesh. Several can share in the same spiritual good and the part of each is in no way diminished. It is only when it goes hand in hand with friendship that erotic love itself is capable of surmounting its natural penchant for jealousy.

Of course, jealous friendships do exist. In fact, they are frequent enough among adolescents, particularly girls. But this does not weaken our argument. If such is the case, it is because at this stage of emotional development there still persists a certain confusion between friendship and love; nor has the sexual instinct fully distinguished itself from the general emotional structure. When adolescents discover love their friendships will cease to be jealous. When jealousy is found in friendship between adults it is usually because on the emotional plane they have not succeeded in overcoming infantilism—unless what they call friendship is in reality love, which they may have unconscious motives for not recognizing as such.

Friendship, like love, demands fidelity. One who is incapable of fidelity is as little apt for friendship as for love. Such fidelity is not always easy and almost always demands a certain effort. Lovers often consider the effort of fidelity a quasi-betrayal of love, for according to the idea they have of their love all feelings and all behavior which it inspires ought to be purely spontaneous. But because of the important role played by the flesh in love a truly spontaneous fidelity generally lasts no longer than the flame of passion. I have often witnessed the astonishment of lovers who had come to realize by experience that their fidelity was far from being able to withstand all trials, that they were capable of being attracted by a third person. But they wrongly concluded that their love had died. Most lovers who are truly faithful realize that such a quality is achieved only with effort and that the awareness of the necessity of effort in no way stains the authenticity of love.

The friend best understands the necessity of this effort. The other's desire to combat every obstacle to the promised fidelity inspires him to redouble his trust. Moreover, the promise of fidelity between friends does not even have to be formulated in words, and the true friend does not demand it. The simple awareness of our friendship for so and so, and the other's consent, already implies an oath of fidelity.

Fidelity between friends is better able than that of lovers to resist the trials of separation, old age and physical and intellectual changes. We may be separated from a friend for long years, in the course of which both of us have changed considerably. Yet when we meet again it generally takes little time and little effort to recreate the feeling of friendship and to take up once again an existential dialogue, as if there had been no interruption. The reason for such fidelity must be sought in the fact that friendship, unlike love, is grounded in the spiritual, in what is permanent in human nature. Our condition of life, our physical appearance, indeed, our ideas and convictions may have changed or developed, but in our deepest selves we are always the same as we were years ago. The fidelity of friendship, as we have described it, can serve as a very valuable argument against a certain phenomenology which pretends that in man, as in the rest of the created universe, there is no permanent substance above and beyond the always changing phenomena and that, because of this, all promise of fidelity is an abuse against existence.

More than love, friendship demands perfect sincerity and rejects falsehood. Strictly speaking, sincerity may suffer an eclipse with lovers without destroying their love. At the moment of carnal ecstasy they may easily, and indeed sincerely, exaggerate the value of their feelings for one another. In such circumstances they are therefore susceptible to promising one another a fidelity that at other times they have no intention of observing. This is not true of friendship. It is precisely this demand of perfect sincerity that makes friendship difficult, if not impossible, for

certain people who have become accustomed to conceal-
ing their true self, supposing that they have indeed become aware of its existence. This is not to say that friends
must give themselves up to incessant confidences of the
kind practiced by adolescents and young working girls.
Rousseau's conception of friendship, entirely grounded on
sentimental effusion, scarcely corresponds to the emotional
needs of adults today. What is important for sincerity in
friendship is that we reveal ourselves to our friend as we
are, without pretense or mask, without affectation or deception. One friend must put himself totally into the
words and actions of the other. However, this demand
must be clearly understood. One who, under pretext of
sincerity, exposes his bad character and faults before his
friends, at the risk of making them suffer, has no right to
the title of sincere friend. It is not enough, either, to dis-
play merely our static self, which is often a lie in itself.
The sincerity of friendship, like friendship itself, appeals
to our emotional dynamisms. It is in "becoming," as we
are in the process of creating ourselves, that we ought to
appear to our friends. One who has renounced the task of
perpetual self-creation becomes incapable of true sincerity
and, therefore, of true friendship.

Let the reader not conclude from this comparison between friendship and love that we depreciate the latter
and exalt the former. We are quite convinced that fidelity
and sincerity are indispensable for that community of love
par excellence which is marriage. But, as we shall see in a
later chapter, if love is to serve as the foundation of this
union it is important that it be allied with friendship.

V

Particular
friendships

WE have said that the most favorable age for the birth of friendship is youth, particularly adolescence. During this time most of the solid friendships that successfully resist the tempests of life are formed. Many adults who suffer from frustrated friendship blame their state upon conditions of life which prevented them from making friends during adolescence or caused them to lose the ones they did make, as though it went without saying (which is not the case) that friends can only be made during adolescence.

Yet many educators take a dim view of friendships between adolescents. In many educational and religious institutions the rule forbids any close relationship between two persons and prescribes that one must be "rarely alone, never with another, always three at least." As soon as two adolescents seek out one another's company and confide in one another they are suspected of equivocal relations, if not homosexuality. The expression "particular friendship" was invented to designate these adolescent friendships and nail them to the pillar of ridicule. As though there could be a friendship that was not "particular"! To deprive young people of this is to deprive them of a most precious emotional experience which more than all others can contribute efficaciously to their psychic maturation, to the liquidation of their narcissism and to an indispensable extroversion.

Of course, friendship often takes on an excessively sentimental character during adolescence, particularly, among young girls. We see them walking hand in hand or with their arms about one another's waist; they frequently embrace and write tender, even passionate letters every day. Although it is not always the fault of the popularizers of Freud, many educators implicitly profess the thesis that all sentimentality and all tenderness are erotic in origin, that "particular friendships" therefore can only be emergent eroticism and, for this reason, immoral.

I do not pretend that more or less overt erotic and homosexual relationships are altogether nonexistent among adolescents. A large number of the homosexuals with whom I have had to deal have, as a matter of fact, begun this practice during adolescence, most frequently in a boarding school. But taking into account the innumerable friendships among young people, these remain rare exceptions, however regrettable we may think them. Should mountain climbing be banned because a few excursionists a year meet death in the mountains? Moreover, according to my information, "particular friendships," as a rule, do not seem to provide the occasion for homosexual deviations in colleges and boarding schools. Most frequently the initiator is an older comrade who is not a friend at all.

It is true that there can often be a troubling element in

manifestations of tenderness between adolescent friends. This is the age of important psychological and physiological changes. The sexual instinct awakens and the need to love and to be loved makes itself felt imperiously. Generally, the adolescent makes no connection between the tender or passionate feelings he has for his friend and the "impure" dreams and desires that assail him. Let us recall the general theory of the libido which seems most in keeping with psychological reality. Emotional energy is in itself undifferentiated, as likely to find expression in friendship as in erotic love. It is only toward the end of adolescence, when sexuality reaches sufficient maturity, that a part of the libido (more or less, depending on the individuals) takes on a clearly erotic coloration. Friendships between adolescents are, as a rule, characterized by confusion, a confusion that is as great as an awareness of specifically sexual realities is less.

One of the worst consequences of badly understood Freudianism is to fear the beginning of homosexuality in the sentimental and tender friendships of adolescence. Provided incompetent educators do not interfere, it is extremely rare for such friendships to inhibit the normal evolution of the sexual instinct toward a partner of the opposite sex. Of course, some carnal agitation is sometimes part of the manifestations of the friendly tenderness that some adolescents practice. But we would be wrong to be overly alarmed. Sometimes adolescent friends talk a good deal about erotic subjects and sometimes "look at one another" and "touch one another." But the desire for pleasure is less a motive than the satisfaction of a curiosity that is altogether normal at this age. Only occasionally, almost by chance, does satisfaction of curiosity lead to a properly erotic satisfaction. In any case, this too exclusive and more or less equivocal kind of friendship between young people generally rights itself without difficulty and without traumatic effect as soon as one or the other, or both, attains a sufficient degree of emotional maturity to be able to love in the erotic sense of the word. Let me give an example from my recent therapeutic experience.

When they were fourteen, Mark and Michael, both students in a religious school, were inseparable friends. During the school holidays they kept up an intense correspondence in which they made truly abusive use of a sentimental vocabulary borrowed from their reading of the Romantic poets. They confided in one another and had promised to "tell all." It is not astonishing, at this age of sexual awakening, that their confidences tended in this direction. They compared the signs of their emerging virility and sometimes touched one another. It seemed a clear-cut case of the kind of "particular friendship" that educators so dread. The two boys, however, sought the advice of one of the priests on the staff. He spoke very frankly of their friendship and its sometimes troubling expressions. The priest was sufficiently intelligent and psychologically informed not to dramatize matters, an attitude that would certainly have had traumatic effects on them.

When Mark was about seventeen, he became infatuated with Michael's sister. Michael, who matured more slowly, was at first very jealous and suffered from the apparent diminution of intimacy with his friend. The desire to equal him, however, stimulated his own emotional growth and soon he too fell in love with a young woman. After the initial perturbations their friendship flourished again, although in a style markedly different from what it formerly had been. Henceforward it was free from excessive mawkishness and sentimentality and became at times rather competitive. Today Mark and Michael are in their thirties. Both are married and have families, but they are still very good friends. They can scarcely recall the troubled period of their adolescent friendship. Yet we may be quite sure that had a priest interfered indiscreetly and tried to separate them, the normal evolution of their emotional life would have been inhibited and perhaps would have suffered serious deviations. If there are dangers and risks in trusting too much to nature, in our experience it is far more dangerous to distrust it unduly.

I do not think it would be helpful to set forth here the many cases of homosexuality that I have known, and which have been caused by the stunting of emotional maturity as a consequence of this kind of clumsiness on the part of educators. To intensify culpability is almost always to run counter to the objective envisaged by the educator. The teacher obviously does not have to approve what may be too sentimental and sensual in the friendship of adolescents. What he must do is speak about it objectively and calmly, and, especially, he must contribute as much as possible to the emotional development of the young. Above all, he must not exhort adolescents to end their friendship under the pretext that everything in it is not perfectly "pure." This would be to go against the very end pursued.

Even less justified is any contempt for the tender friendships between young girls. Their erotic awakening generally comes later than that of boys. It is as a result of masculine initiative that most young girls become aware of their sensuality. It little matters whether psychoanalysts are right or wrong in regarding as nascent eroticism the sensual and sentimental expressions that characterize almost all friendships between young girls. It would be absurd to treat them as potential lesbians. Even very exclusive and jealous friendships between them almost always become normal as soon as they reach sufficient maturity to be sensitive to masculine attention. The most that can be said is that such expressions of tenderness indicate a desire and the unconscious expectation of loving a man and being loved by him. The small percentage of girls who do indulge in sapphic deviation rarely do so with a friend of their own age. The initiator is invariably an older person, someone already confirmed in the practice, as I have explained in Chapter V of *The Psychology of Loving*.

From a psychological point of view, the only real danger in "particular friendships" among adolescents is the risk they run of becoming narcissistic. The consequence can more or less seriously hinder their extroversion, their adaptation to the outside world. To palliate this danger educators ought not thwart particular friendships but see to it that they become integrated into larger groups and communities. It is good for every adolescent to have his friend, but he should also have chums and comrades. Youth movements, particularly the Boy Scouts, seem to us an ideal framework for the development of friendship among adolescents. Parents who prefer their child to spend all his time in the company of a friend carefully chosen by them commit a grave psychological and pedagogical error.

VI

Friendship between men

THEORETICALLY at least, as we have noted, friendship can blossom between people of all conditions, all ages and both sexes. We must not idealize it to the point where it appears accessible only to an elite. For friendship, it is sufficient that at least some of the fundamental conditions we have analyzed in the preceding chapters be realized. Seldom are they all combined in any given friendship. Yet it remains true that not all friendships reach the same degree of perfection; some are better than others. If "true friendship" is encountered more frequently among one category of people than another, it is, in our opinion, because of the level of psychological development as much as the sociological conditions.

Most of the notable examples of great friendships are those between men. The Bible narrates the extraordinary friendship between Jonathan, the eldest son of King Saul, and the young David, whom Saul suspected of desiring his throne and whom he pursued as a rebel. Jonathan joyfully sacrificed his right to the throne in the name of friend-

ship and when he died in battle, the sorrow of the poet
David brought forth very beautiful words to mourn him.
All of Christ's friends explicitly mentioned in the Gospel
were men: John, Lazarus, the Apostles and disciples in
general. Even Judas, who betrayed him in the Garden of
Gethsemane, is called "friend" by Jesus; yet He never
used this term in addressing Mary Magdalen or the sisters
of Lazarus, even though He was frequently their guest.
The same is true of the friendships spoken of in Plato's
Socratic dialogues and in innumerable other works of antiquity, not only Greek, but Latin, Arabic and Oriental
works as well. Closer to us, with what sorrowful affection
does Montaigne speak of his friend La Boétie. The pre-
mature death of the latter left him inconsolable. This loss
seemed to him infinitely greater than the loss of his wife
and children. It would be easy to multiply examples of
great and beautiful friendships between men, examples
drawn from literature or observed in the world about us.

Since the fact of friendship between men, and the important existential role which it plays, is incontestable do
we have the right to conclude that there can be true
friendship only between men? Many authors have thought
this to be the case. Plato, Aristotle, Cicero, Augustine,
Montaigne and many others explicitly affirm that authentic friendship is possible only between those of the
masculine sex. They support this opinion by their experience. Too, modern opinion is quite disposed to accept
this thesis. Only men are thought capable of the disinterest,
seriousness and fidelity which friendship demands. In
modern terminology it would be said that only men possess sufficient emotional maturity for friendship.

The thesis presented in these terms seems overstated to

us. We spoke earlier of friendship between children and adolescents and will soon have occasion to speak of the existence of friendship between many other categories of people. To restrict authentic friendship to men limits the notion of friendship excessively and makes it possible only for an elite. That friendship among the elite, such as between Jonathan and David, Christ and the Apostle John, Montaigne and La Boétie, appears more sublime than among the ordinary run of humanity is incontestable. But this is no argument against the important existential function friendship also plays at lesser levels.

What is certain is that friendship plays an indispensable role in the life of men at all levels of their intellectual and emotional development. The saints and ascetics, who feel bound to renounce love and most other earthly joys, generally do not renounce friendship. Christ himself, as we have seen, had friends. I know of many men who find much pleasure in feminine company, especially when the women are spiritual and beautiful. And yet this companionship can rarely replace their friendship with other men. Most men feel "truly themselves" only in the presence of other men. They speak and act very differently with their male friends, however intimate may be their relations with women. When a male friend fails them, most men feel genuinely frustrated despite their success with women, perhaps even despite an authentic "great love." Love itself is no durable substitute for friendship with other men. Many young wives are puzzled by the imperious need their husbands have of continuing their relationships with male friends. They take offense, become jealous and consider themselves insufficiently loved. In reality, there is no contradiction between a man's love for his wife and his friendship with other men. They are two complementary orders of existential communication. It is my experience that, generally speaking, men who break with their friends to please their wives or have no friends are much less stable and fulfilled in love than others. Friendship enriches love; it does not threaten it.

It is certain that some masculine friendships are more or less tainted with homosexual eroticism. With the Greeks of the Golden Age this was especially the case and today we are slightly embarrassed in citing those beautiful pages of Plato, for example, to illustrate friendship among men. Yet it would nonetheless be a serious and quite illegitimate simplification to conclude that all friendship is a more or less well-sublimated homosexual love. The most authentic masculine friendships I have known involved men in whom even the most Freudian psychoanalyst would be hard put to find any indication of sexual inversion. Moreover, friendships between homosexuals bear little resemblance to the kind of friendship we have described and defined. It is jealous and capricious and brings more trouble than peace and joy. As for the Greeks of Plato's time, I do not think that the homosexual practices then in usage authorize us to judge negatively the sublime things they wrote about friendship. A certain confusion existed; but not all values were compromised. In our opinion it would be psychologically true to say that their friendship existed not *because* of their homosexual love but rather *despite* it.

VII

Feminine
friendships

No one denies the possibility of friendship between men or the important role it plays in their lives. On the other hand, we are often skeptical about a genuine friendship between women. Many men take it for granted that women are too vain and too selfish to be capable of a lasting and solid friendship. They are, of course, aware of the existence of passionate attachments between adolescents, but they refuse to see in them the seeds of friendship. It is understood that two young girls who embrace one another with tenderness, walk arm in arm and whisper confidences to one another are seeking from each other, more or less consciously, a substitute for erotic love. Friendship between boys, who exchange more blows than confidences, would be the only nonequivocal model of friendship between adolescents. While boys who are friends avoid sentimental expressions of affection and readily discuss general ideas, friendship between girls is considered by men, rightly or wrongly, excessively intimate. The same is true of all feminine friendships, the age and the condition of the partners notwithstanding.

But men are not alone in stubbornly doubting the possibility of authentic friendship between women. Many women themselves do so much more categorically. Many intellectual women have told me that they envy men for their ability to form friendships which give them a joy forever forbidden to women. Simone de Beauvoir, who is considered the most competent spokesman for "modern woman," declares peremptorily in *The Second Sex:* "Women are comrades of captivity for each other, they help one another support their prison, even to prepare for their escape; but the liberator will come from the masculine world." This means that there may be a certain complicity among women, but never friendship. If two women act like friends they are immediately suspected by other women of carrying on more or less unspeakable relations. The suspicion of lesbianism is strengthened if it is a question of friendship between two single women, especially when they live together.

It cannot be denied that more or less overtly lesbian deviations exist among women. There is no doubt that sapphic loves exist, although they are infinitely less frequent than gossiping tongues would have it. But homosexual relations also exist among men, probably more so than among women. The fideists of psychoanalysis excepted, however, no one would think of arguing from this against the possibility and the reality of very authentic masculine friendships in which eroticism plays absolutely no role. I believe we can say more. Whether it be a question of men or women, the more or less conscious presence of homosexual factors in their relationships in no way authorizes us to deny or doubt true friendship between the same persons. In the human psyche things rarely achieve the simplicity of rational categories.

I have been acquainted with a certain number of feminine friendships in which the sapphic played an effective role. In the great majority of cases it was totally unconscious. The friendship of Theresa and‑ Ann lent itself to such a malevolent interpretation, and they were the laughingstock of their neighbors. Theresa manifested all the signs of a masculine kind of girl: moustache, large shoulders, a deep voice, and so on. These symptoms were accentuated by her markedly masculine manner of dressing and by the cigar she smoked incessantly. Ann, on the other hand, had an air of almost infantile femininity. The two girls knew each other when they were students and rapidly became inseparable friends. Since they chose the same profession they found it natural to live together, for economic reasons and to be less alone. They walked about arm in arm and Theresa's customary attitude toward Ann was that of a well-bred gentleman for his sweetheart. In short, the appearances were such that I had no doubt about the sapphic character of this friendship.

Then one day Theresa spoke to me about certain professional difficulties she was having. Soon afterward Ann consulted me and I became the confidant of both. In the course of their analysis it became clear that the psychophysiological virility of Theresa and the infantile femininity of Ann was an important determinant in the birth of their friendship. Ann needed to be protected and coddled, but her infantilism went hand in hand with her fear of men; a virile woman friend suited her perfectly. As for Theresa, she felt herself in perpetual competition with men and consequently refused to seek from them the emotional warmth she needed; the *petite* Ann fully satisfied her need to devote herself to someone weaker. But both were quite unaware of these motivations in their friendship. For the ten years they lived together there was never anything specifically erotic in their relations; their strict religious superego prevented them from even thinking that they could be anything but friends to each other. In the course of treatment they became conscious of the "platonically sapphic" nature of their friendship. Must they then renounce it? I firmly dissuaded them from doing so. I had no doubt whatsoever as to the positive value of the friendship in the life of these two women. Moreover, psychosynthesis had effected a certain equilibrium in both, and consequently the risks of a lesbian deviation of their friendship was henceforward greatly diminished. It pertains to psychosynthesis to tend not to destroy but to correct what is deviate. Whether it be a question of friendship, love, religious faith or moral principles we never try to destroy them but only to eliminate their neurotic motivations.

To understand these kinds of friendship properly it is necessary to refer once again to our general theory of the libido, or emotional energy, which is by nature not sexual but undifferentiated. When for some reason or other, whether a lack of opportunity or neurotic inhibitions (as in the case of the two women we have just discussed), this emotional energy cannot express itself in erotic love, it flows quite normally and more or less abundantly toward that other form of emotional communion which is friendship. Thus there is nothing abnormal or immoral in the fact that friendship between two single women, that is to say women who are erotically frustrated, should resemble in some respects erotic love more than a friendship between two women who are erotically fulfilled. The same is true, although with appreciable differences, for men. This explains, for example, the intense intimacy of friendships which are formed in prison camps or among political deportees. Men in these conditions, frustrated for lack of love, direct their libidinal energies toward friendship. Nor can we characterize, in the great majority of cases, such friendships as "sexual" in any way.

In the case of women, in our opinion it would be unpardonably cruel to wish to forbid or discredit their friendly intimacy under the pretext that such friendships consummate a libido which "normally" ought to find expression in love relations between men and women. It is far more dangerous for psychic balance to let libidinal energies lie dormant. I have always encouraged sexually frustrated women to form as intense and intimate friendships with other women as possible; at the same time I instruct them how to palliate certain lesbian deviations that might occur and of which their moral conscience would disapprove. While a repressed libido can bring about neurosis, or at least an emotional sterility, sublimation in friendship enables it to make the life of women (who without it would be lamentable derelicts) beautiful and fruitful. If the "old maid" of former days was so susceptible to ridicule by reason of her small manias and the narrowness of her ideas it was, as far as we have been able to determine, less because she was sexually frustrated than because the kind of life she led prevented her from forming sublimating friendships. The case is different for many single women today, especially when they have the opportunity of engaging in professional activity that is suitable to their tastes. In any case, it is high time we ceased casting the stones of stupid jokes and suppressed smiles at those women who live together as friends and find in their mutual affection the strength and the courage necessary to confront the difficult battles of life.

It would be wrong, however, to make feminine friendship the privilege of single women. We noted in the preceding chapter that men who are perfectly happy and fulfilled in their married life experience the need and the benefits of friendship with other men and that everyone accepts this as normal. Why should it not be the same for married women? To their own detriment too many young wives believe that married love is enough to satisfy totally and definitively, their emotional needs, and they look upon any other form of existential communication almost as a kind of betrayal. They thus neglect or break off the friendships they had before marriage and at the same time become jealous of the friendships which their husbands continue to cultivate. Little by little, sometimes only after several years of marriage, these women become aware of the emptiness in their life caused by the absence of friendship. I have often observed how efficaciously a wife's friendship with another woman can serve conjugal love. A woman who expects everything from her husband generally soon becomes a burden to him. He has problems and worries that he thinks, rightly or wrongly, he ought not or cannot share with his wife, if for no other reason than the desire not to upset her. He has friends and centers of interest that are not those of his wife. Her emotional exclusivity thus often engenders a painful tension that can more or less seriously compromise conjugal love. This tension generally disappears as soon as the wife begins to communicate on a basis of friendship with another woman.

Our experience indicates that friendship between a married and a single woman is especially enriching for both of them. It is in effect psychically very fulfilling for the single woman to share through her friend in home life, in its joys and worries. It is particularly good for single women no longer living with their families to be received into a family as friends, to be able to interest themselves in the children and so forth. The fear that such intimacy with home life can make some single women more sorrowfully aware of what is lacking in their own lives is not without foundation, but this inconvenience seems to me largely compensated for by the emotional enrichment they are likely to receive.

Still more can such a friendship benefit a married woman, especially when she is not active in a professional or extrafamilial capacity. Intimacy with a woman who works professionally, and for this reason has more contacts with the outside world, who is normally more interested than a mother or wife in what is going on in the world and has more time to read and participate in different cultural activities, can provide the married woman with an opportunity to broaden her horizons beyond the confines of domestic life. Stimulated and enriched by her friend, she will be better able to communicate with her husband and his friends and not feel so completely left out.

There is no reason to presume that the average woman is incapable of authentic friendship. Those who hold this view generally refer to the past. But even supposing great friendships between women were rare in the past, it would be absurd to attribute this to some structural impossibility. Woman's nature is not something static, definitively fixed once and for all, any more than is that of man or of the universe as a whole. In former times woman's circumstances of life made it difficult, if not impossible, to live the kind of friendship celebrated by Plato or Montaigne and about which we are speaking in these pages. With some magnificent exceptions, women have only recently attained an awareness of themselves as persons. They were brought up and lived to serve man. They expected their total fulfillment from him alone and believed that he had a unique need of their tenderness, of a good mother for his children and a good mistress for his household. Those who did not marry were destined, in our western world and Christian tradition, for the convent. Or they vegetated in the shadow of the home of a brother or a married sister. Of course, women of the so-called upper class, those who had plenty of leisure time, associated with one another in the past even more than they do today. As proof of this we have only to refer to the literature of the seventeenth century or the novels of Proust. But the field of interest and preoccupations of these women was extremely restricted. They gossiped about trivialities unless, as is current in the women's quarters of Islamic countries, they sought the affection from one another that was generally lacking in their relations with their husbands. It is all too easy to understand how such friendships lent themselves more to irony and humor than to admiration.

It is evident that the conditions of life, both sociological and psychological, of most women today bear little resemblance to that of such women. They take the same difficult studies as their male comrades and frequently practice the same professions. They are interested in philosophy, literature, art and religion, as well as politics and economics, often with more passion than men. Consequently, empty gossip no longer satisfies them in their relations with one another. They are disposed to conduct that kind of dialogue in which true communication is the very essence of friendship. The principal obstacle to authentic friendship between women is the survival of the prejudices of another age.

VIII

Friendship between
men and women

IN the preceding chapters we analyzed friendship between persons of the same sex. Many moralists and psychologists think there can be friendship only between members of the same sex and suspect that friendships between men and women are more or less a disguise of erotic love. Are they right? There are many examples in which a man and woman have thought their friendship was "pure" until they fell into one another's arms. From appearances it would seem that they were mistaken about the real nature of their feelings for one another. In my various books on depth psychology I have exposed and analyzed several such loves which dared not admit their true name. Suffice it to give here a particularly typical example.

Andrew and Helen had been married for five years; from every point of view it was a good marriage. One day Helen's girlhood friend Elizabeth came to live in the same city. Helen perhaps was too happy to receive her friend into her lovely home and show off her happiness before a single girl of thirty. She invited her frequently, to the point of annoying her husband, who preferred to spend some time alone with his wife and children. Helen continued to call her husband's attention to Elizabeth's intelligence and culture. Gradually Andrew began to notice that his wife's friend was a "superior woman"; he began to talk to her while his wife busied herself with domestic tasks. For several years a very beautiful and intense friendship united the three. They spent Sundays and summer holidays together. One day, however, Helen discovered that the other two were seeing one another separately. She felt some jealousy but thought it unworthy of their beautiful friendship; she did what she could to repress it. It came as a shock when her husband told her that he now loved Elizabeth, had been her lover for some time and wanted to divorce her and marry Elizabeth. Helen blamed herself for her imprudence. But she wrongly accused her friend of deceit, of having schemed to win her husband's affections. Elizabeth believed in the "purity" of her friendship with Andrew until the end. Andrew himself became aware of the progressive metamorphosis of friendship into love only very late, when "almost by chance" he began to embrace his friend more tenderly and frequently. This took place after certain conflicts and deceptions in his relations with his wife. Thus, without the sincerity of any of the friends being diminished, this friendship between a man and a woman led to disaster, to the destruction of the harmony of a family. And I have no doubt that many of my women readers will be tempted to conclude that they must not be as naïve as Helen.

Most frequently it is in a climate of such loyalty and good faith that Eros enters into friendship between a man and a woman. Often enough a man proposes only friendship to a woman because he imagines she would reject his amorous advances. Sometimes he traps himself as well as the other. "Since I cannot be her lover," he says, "at least I can have her as a friend." He may even try very sincerely to be only a friend, without, however, letting any opportune occasion pass to attain his first objective. Women who consent to this kind of friendship are generally of greater good faith than men, especially if they are not experienced in love. According to our knowledge of these matters, particularly suspect is the friendship which married men of a certain age offer young girls, usually their secretaries, under the pretext of being consoled for the misunderstandings they suffer from their wives. Subjective sincerity is not always lacking in such cases, but in reality such men are looking for a kind of affection that is not friendship.

Can we conclude from the very real difficulties and failures we have just described that friendship between men and women is impossible? We do not think so. There are failures; but there are as many successes. We could give many examples of such friendships which succeeded beyond any question. We think first of all of the great and universally known friendships which embellished the lives of so many saints and proved existentially to be of extraordinary fecundity. Clare and Francis of Assisi, Teresa of Ávila and John of the Cross, Jeanne de Chantal and Francis de Sales realized such great things for the glory of God at least partially because of their friendships. That such friendships are very much in keeping with the Christian spirit is proved by the fact that they were lauded by early hagiographers. The latter admired the friendship between Jerome and Saint Paula and attributed a similar friendship, although perhaps with less evidence, to Ambrose and Monica, the mother of St. Augustine. It seems to me that the magnificent success and the spiritual fecundity of such friendships absolves friendship between men and women of its few failures; in any case, we are not so impressed by failures as to declare such friendship impossible.

The great saints and mystics are not the only ones to have succeeded in such friendships. Michelangelo and Vittoria Colonna were not exactly saints, any more than numerous other men and women we know from ancient, medieval and modern literature. Even in our own age, which is so fascinated by eroticism, I know many men and women who are neither saints nor heroes but find the greatest and purest joys of their lives in their mutual friendship. The friendship between Andrew, Helen and Elizabeth might well have succeeded; I know of similar ones that go on for years without the least failure.

In certain cases the absence of the erotic element in a friendship between a man and a woman is facilitated by many factors. Alice, a woman of exceptional intellectual and moral qualities, was a close friend of Henry for several years; there was never any question about the nature of their sentiments. As a young girl Alice suffered from poliomyelitis, which crippled her rather severely. Otherwise, it is quite possible that Henry would have loved her erotically. But the point I wish to make is that a long, beautiful and fruitful friendship was established between a man and a woman. In several other similar cases no physical obstacle to eroticism existed. The couples were friends rather than lovers for moral reasons; or because one or the other, or both, were erotically committed to another person. A man or woman who is unhappy in his or her home life is not suited for this kind of friendship, while those who are happy in love can indulge in it with far less risk of deviation.

To try to establish a friendship with a person of the opposite sex on a purely spiritual basis is to invite painful disillusionment. The great pessimist La Bruyère himself held that friendship between a man and a woman was possible without risk to the masculinity of the one or the femininity of the other. St. Francis of Sales, who personally experienced one of the best-known and most beautiful friendships with a woman, recognized that the senses play a certain role even in the most spiritual of friendships. As a matter of fact, our first impression of the other is mediated through the senses. We have only to read the correspondence of St. Francis with Jeanne de Chantal to be convinced that both sentimentality and sensuality were present in this saintly friendship.

In such friendships Eros is certainly not absent but is so perfectly sublimated that we rightly consider them "noncarnal," in the current sense of the word "carnal." As for "ordinary" men and women, they are well advised to become fully aware of the role Eros plays in their friendship. The old adage: "He who tries to be an angel will become a beast," is applicable to our problem. There can clearly be no question of repressing Eros, only of sublimating it. The word "sublimation" must be understood in a sense not given it by Freudian psychology. The true emotional nature of man is not limited to instinctive impulses alone. There is nothing antinatural in trying to direct the emotional energy of these impulses, whether totally or partially, toward more specifically human faculties. We have tried to show in other works (*cf. The Authentic Morality* and *Teilhard and the Faith of Men*) that man's nature is less in his animal past than in the increasingly spiritualized future toward which he tends. The sublimation of the libido, that is to say its adduction toward activities which are less carnal and more spiritual, is quite in accord with a human nature in process. Such sublimation, which is perfectly legitimate, is in practice more or less realizable depending on the emotional and spiritual maturity of individuals. The nuances between the "loving friendships" which the troubadours cultivated (in which the presence of Eros was scarcely concealed) and the friendship of Francis de Sales with Jeanne de Chantal are almost infinite.

Whatever the dangers, it is our firm conviction that friendship between man and woman is not an impossible ideal. But it can only be realized between persons who have attained a relatively high degree of spirituality, persons whose so-called higher values are very much in evidence. Even more than in friendship between those of the same sex, it is indispensable here that the communion of friends be effected in the pursuit of the same ideal, in the realization of a common work. Even then there is no guarantee against the more or less disorderly intrusion of erotic passion. However, the benefits of such a friendship are so great that it is not, in our opinion, imprudent to accept with full knowledge the risks it exposes us to. Further, nothing truly precious can be accomplished in life without the risk of deviation and error. He who risks nothing will never rise above the banality of everyday existence. Are we too optimistic in presuming that the progress of the noosphere and the emotional maturation of mankind are in the process of being accomplished rapidly enough to permit an increasingly greater number of men and women to benefit by such friendships?

A friendship without Eros among young people of opposite sexes is, in our opinion, practically impossible. Their experience of life is insufficient to enable them to effect the necessary sublimations. They do not know themselves at all well and know others still less. While waiting for greater emotional and spiritual maturity, let them be content with the beautiful and open relations of camaraderie or of a group friendship which we shall later have occasion to laud.

IX

Friendship
within marriage

In the previous chapter we discussed friendship between men and women who for different reasons wish to or must renounce erotic relations. Does this mean that friendship and love are irreconcilable by nature? This, for all practical purposes, is the opinion of a La Bruyère, and Montaigne says that the soul of women who marry is not strong enough to bear the weight of friendship. The experiences and theses of these two great moralists are in accord with the thought and practices of the ancients. The Greeks practiced friendship with the hetaera, those free women who were often very knowledgeable in poetry, art and philosophy, but they would never have dreamed of seeking this kind of spiritual communion with their wives. In Japan geishas play a similar role. It is true that the Greeks, the Japanese and all those who think that their wives are unworthy or incapable of friendship generally do not marry for passionate love. They love their wives "rationally" or for the sake of duty.

Yet friendship and conjugal love are by no means

mutually exclusive. To our knowledge Plutarch was the first to say that the wife is as capable and worthy, if not more so, of friendship with a man as the hetaera. If in former times such friendship has been relatively rare, it is more common today as consciences mature and the conditions and motivations of marriage change.

There is first of all the case, more and more frequent today, of marriage between friends. Thus, as we indicated, mature men today do not establish friendships with the hetaera or geishas or their homologues. Friends meet at the university, in political or social circles; it is thus that they become partners in an existential dialogue, that they become friends. Later they may fall in love. Since no insurmountable exterior obstacle exists they quite naturally decide to marry. Love evidently in no way damages their friendship nor does the latter diminish the ardor of their love. Quite the contrary, love and friendship mutually nourish and enrich one another.

It happens only too frequently that those who marry on the basis of physical attraction alone realize after a time of ordinary living that they have nothing to say to one another, that they are strangers to one another. It is the nature of erotic love to be very intense at first, but it tends to diminish, if not disappear altogether, after it has been satisfied. It is more like a straw fire than a true flame. Seldom does a purely carnal passion resist the inevitable difficulties and disenchantments of daily life. The divorce rate is highest among such "marriages of love"; frequently they end after only one or two years.

The case of marriages based on solid friendship is evidently quite different. Even when they are not erotically successful, harmony between the couple is not destroyed.

They continue to communicate with each other as they did when they were friends, before the birth of love. They know one another in depth and do not let their superficial faults upset them. They have something to talk about outside of the conjugal bed. But, above all, erotic love itself generally acquires a greater intensity and longer duration among married couples who are also friends.

To illustrate these considerations let me discuss two cases which I have observed closely.

Edward and Frances met at a surprise party. They danced together all night and immediately became en-amored of one another. They became lovers the same night. Some months later, when Frances became pregnant, they married. At the time they knew very little about one another, having scarcely discussed their tastes and con-victions. They got along well sexually and this made them feel quite happy together. But married life, unfortunately, is not lived entirely in bed. Shortly after their marriage their silence in one another's presence was almost total. Edward took up with his old friends and showed no desire to introduce his wife to them. Under these conditions conjugal fidelity lost all meaning; both embarked upon extramarital affairs. Their sexual relations remained fre-quent, although they were more an expression of sado-masochism than of love, and this alone prevented them from separating definitively. After seven years of marriage Frances came to see me; not yet thirty, she had suffered a severe nervous breakdown and her husband had lost all courage to continue fighting life's battles and was obsessed with the thought of suicide.

Of course, not all such marriages in which true friend-ship is lacking break up so dramatically. Nonetheless, this extreme case is in some sense typical and teaches us an important lesson. This is all the more true in that both of the persons involved were characters of some depth.

When I first knew Martin and Susan some twenty years ago they were both students and actively engaged in a religious movement at the university. She was the more intellectual of the two; he the more practical; they thus complemented one another admirably and often worked together. She initiated him to a deeper philosophical and spiritual life. He taught her the pleasures of music and, to some extent, those of athletics. In short, theirs was an exemplary friendship in which there was no trace of flirtation, the more so in that Susan clearly lacked sophistication and, indeed, the charm indispensable to a young girl. It was only some five or six years later, when they had both embarked upon professional life, that they decided to marry. I was somewhat skeptical about the chances for the emotional success of this union. There seemed to be very little erotic passion between the two friends and in those days I attached much more importance to it than I do today as a preliminary condition for a happy marriage. Susan and Martin have now been married for fifteen years. They are no longer young and have a large family. Their friendship is as authentic as it was when they were students; or rather, it has deepened and been enriched by the joys and sorrows they have shared over the years. On the erotic level their beginnings were difficult enough, as they readily admit, but friendship triumphed over these difficulties and gradually they effected a harmony in their sex life. Considering the past and present emotional situation of this couple, I do not think it presumptuous to suppose that if for some reason—sickness or old age, for example—they had one day to renounce erotic communion the solid bonds of friendship would continue to solder their union.

Not all marriages between friends and without initial erotic passion succeed so well. Nonetheless, this example illustrates that friendship is an excellent basis for love and that the two mutually strengthen one another.

I could also speak of an old married couple whom I know well. They have reached the age when erotic love is no longer important. But the profound friendship they have always enjoyed constitutes an unbreakable bond between them and embellishes the evening of their life. Their intellectual and spiritual exchanges are still intense, and they are still capable of enthusiasm and discuss passionately many subjects. I like to compare this husband and wife with another old couple who were very much in love when they were young but who were never friends. They can no longer tolerate one another and mutually contribute to the sufferings of their old age.

Normally, friendship ought to precede love just as it ought to survive it. But I know several married couples who were not friends before they were married. Passion or common family or social interests formed the basis of their marriage. Friendship was born afterward. Although they were not conscious of it in the beginning, they had enough in common to become friends. It was common enough in the time of our grandparents, at least in the upper echelons of society, for marriages to be "arranged" between the parents, thus excluding all possibility of the young people's knowing each other in any depth. It was often the case that in the beginning there was neither love nor friendship; nonetheless, one or both blossomed after marriage. The old couple I mentioned above fall into this category.

Nor is the birth of friendship in a marriage of passion a priori impossible, provided the couple do not become discouraged as soon as the flame of the senses which they took to be the passion of their lives flickers. As they come to know one another more deeply, they may well reach a communion of friendship. The most serious obstacle to the birth of friendship in such cases is the overestimation of the love that motivates marriage. Too many young people believe in the eternity of their love. They do not try to know one another better, and they attach no importance to the fact that they do not have much to say to one another. They more or less consciously believe that the flesh is a sufficiently solid reality to bind them together forever. When, after some months or years, the intoxication of the flesh fades it is generally too late for friendship to be born. The accumulation of disappointments of every kind will have made them unavailable to one another; the passion that blinded them will have precluded the possibility of self-knowledge.

X

Friendship
between parents
and children

THE "bond of blood" is not a necessary condition for the
birth of friendship. The latter is a reality of the spiritual
order, and it is common knowledge that spiritual parenthood is not always identical with parenthood according to
the flesh, just as the latter does not imply any affinity of
spirits. There are many families in which there is no
spiritual communion, no community of ideas or interests.
True friendship does of course exist between members of
the same family, between brothers and sisters, for example,
but it is safe to say that it is born not because of their
blood relationship but in spite of it.

What makes friendship between brothers and sisters
generally more difficult than between strangers is the kind
of shame that often governs their relationship. Because
they live under the same roof they wrongly believe that
they know one another in depth and therefore do not dare
manifest toward each other precisely what is most beauti-

ful and most generous in their aspirations. To this must be
added the small trials of daily life. Not infrequently
brothers and sisters come to know one another through
a third party or through associations to which they belong.
I once knew two brothers who had very little respect
for one another. When they were about twenty-five they
found that they had both become members of the same
political party. They were surprised to discover the
spiritual community which existed between them and that,
from an early age, they had shared the same ideals of
generosity. They then became close friends.

In adolescence, friendship between brothers and sisters
does not always seem to be desirable, or rather, is is desirable only under certain conditions. There is a risk of becoming imprisoned by too close a family circle. This favors
narcissism and can become an obstacle to the extroversion
necessary to adolescents. Thus friendship within the family
ought always be complemented by friendships outside the
family. It is best that brothers and sisters become friends,
not within the family itself, but through the mediation of
the outside world. In this manner too, the dangers of juve-
nile narcissism are more easily overcome. Should parents
notice that their children's relations are too exclusive of
the outside world they ought to become concerned and
seek ways of encouraging them to come into contact with
other young people.

In the not-too-distant past there was no question of
friendship between parents and children. The father was,
or at least wanted to be, the head, the representative of
God and country, to whom the children owed obedience
and respect. Very few parents attempted to engage in true
dialogue with their children, even after they had become

adults. If a son thirty years old dared contradict his father on some point he was immediately accused of disrespect. I still know of some well-established families in which the father alone talks at the family table. The mother in such families generally protected and cherished her children but did not truly communicate with them. No personal or intimate question was ever discussed between parents and children. Questions of sexual initiation, for example, were never brought up. On the eve of marriage the most a mother would say to her daughter, and this with great shame and hesitancy, was that she ought to submit to whatever her husband demanded of her because there was no sin "in that" between a husband and wife. The father, when he desired to be particularly "open," told his son on such occasions how to avoid having a baby too soon. Today many people over forty and even some who are younger have told me they never had any real communication with their parents, that they never spoke man-to-man or woman-to-woman about religion or politics, art or literature. Their father was generally content to proclaim more or less peremptorily his ideas without admitting that one of his children might wish to disagree or have ideas of his own. I remember the consternation, indeed, the scandal, of a certain well-to-do family when they learned that their son had belonged to the Communist party for some thirty years. They never suspected that such ideas existed in their household. And for good reason! It was formerly the case, and is often enough today, that a son will join a revolutionary party or movement less out of conviction than as a reaction against paternal authoritarianism, although most frequently he is not conscious of the real motives for his action. On the religious level, believing parents demanded that their children "practice" the faith without worrying too much about the state of their soul or conscience.

Today more and more parents desire true friendship with their children. I know of several families in which such friendship exists between parents in their forties and children between the ages of sixteen and twenty to the mutual benefit of both. We must recognize, however, that in the present development of the human conscience, the realization of such friendship is not always easy.

I am thinking of a woman who succeeded in becoming friends with her oldest daughter. Unfortunately, their friendship was clearly founded on a complicity against the husband and father, whom neither could tolerate. Moreover, it was the mother who communicated to her daughter her feelings of hatred and hostility toward her husband. I am also thinking of a man who never had the slightest spiritual communion with his wife and who, by way of compensation, got along magnificently with his daughter. Another father was close to his adolescent son; they shared many athletic interests and visited nightclubs together; but this was principally because he wanted to remove his son from the influence of his wife, which the father considered harmful and which had considerably interfered with his own life. In all of these cases, and we could prolong the list, friendship with the child was a compensation to one of the parents for the emotional emptiness of his conjugal life. And from this alone such friendships were improperly motivated. There is no doubt about the harm this can cause the children. True friendship must be *for* and not *against* someone or something.

Friendship between parents and children, more than

between brothers and sisters, risks becoming an obstacle to their necessary extroversion, to their orientation toward the exterior world in which they must realize their vocation as men and women. This is true of the best of friendships, and still more so of those reactive and compensatory friendships we have given examples of above.

These very real dangers must not, however, be construed as a warning against friendship between parents and children, still less as a condemnation. Quite the contrary. We have drawn attention to the pitfalls only because we are firmly persuaded of the existential fecundity of this kind of friendship, and this as much for the parents as for the children. But its chances of success are enhanced by an awareness of the difficulties. And the chief responsibility for avoiding obstacles and overcoming difficulties belongs, obviously, to the parents.

As we have said, friendship between one of the parents and one of the children ought not be on any condition, not even unconsciously, a complicity against another parent or one of the children. Those parents most likely to succeed in establishing an authentic friendship with their children are evidently those who not only love one another but are also friends. Moreover, this friendship must not be exclusive but must favor friendships between the children and others outside of the family and closer to them in age. Finally, if such friendship is to succeed it is indispensable that the parents deliberately renounce all authoritarianism, all desire to dominate. They must encourage in their children, insofar as they can, the sentiments of equality and responsibility. This evidently does not exclude that authority which parents must have. But authority is not the same as authoritarianism.

Let us admit that the realization of all the conditions indispensable to the promotion of family friendship is not at all easy. Yet we are in a position to affirm, on the basis of numerous examples known to us, that it is in no way impossible. And the results that we may legitimately expect are certainly worth the effort required.

XI

Friendship
between master
and disciple

FOR a master, having a disciple is quite different from having a student. We can be someone's student without recognizing him as a master. The student learns what the other teaches without necessarily adhering to his ideas or to the spirit of his teaching. Between master and disciple, on the other hand, there is always a certain spiritual kinship, a certain emotional rapport. Bergson told me one day that to be his disciple it was not at all necessary to profess the essential theses of his philosophy; it was sufficient to experience the same love as he for the truth and the same passion to seek it out. Undoubtedly there were many among his students who docilely repeated the master's opinions without being his disciples. They followed the letter rather than the spirit of their master's work. When we speak of friendship between master and disciple it is impossible not to think first of all of the magnificent narratives in the Gospel which show us Christ among His disciples and friends. He did not teach like the scribes in the synagogue who pretended to transmit faithfully the wisdom of Holy Scripture and Tradition. Christ addressed the hearts of His disciples more than their minds. The evidence indicates that He loved them and was loved by them. They lived together, took their meals in common, often spent the night under the stars and possessed nothing of their own. The evangelists report some of the many conversations that took place between Christ and His disciples in the three years of His public life. At least three quarters of evangelical teaching consists of these friendly dialogues between the Master and his Disciples. This explains the often fragmentary and sometimes paradoxical character of the Gospels.

Another sublime example of friendship between master and disciple is furnished by the life of Socrates. It would be difficult to find a greater example of this kind of friendship than the last conversations of Socrates with his disciples in his prison cell. There was deep emotion on both sides; yet Socrates was always the master and the disciples never forgot who they were.

Were we to choose a text which best glorifies this kind of friendship, we would probably choose the one in which Plato speaks of his friend Dio. But we would have to abstract from the context of homosexuality which somewhat lessens this friendship in our eyes. We would have to situate ourselves within the Greek morality of the age to understand that the friendship between Plato and Dio is nonetheless a friendship between master and disciple, very different from the kind of friendship which Gide and his pale emulators promoted.

In the *Confessions*, especially in the chapters consecrated to the community of friends about him at Cassiacum, St.

Augustine also gives us a fine example of friendship between master and disciple. And there are many other similar examples.

A master is rare enough, even among the most eminent savants and professors. The master, as much as the father who wishes to be friends with his son, must renounce authoritarianism, all spirit of domination and what is justly called "paternalism." It is not a simple matter for a student to become the friend-disciple of a master. If the master must unite prestige and humility with profound respect for the respective personalities of his disciples, one can become an authentic friend-disciple only on the condition that he is already sufficiently structured as a person and has already attained a relatively elevated degree of intellectual and emotional maturity. Otherwise, all effort at profound communication with a strong personality, which a master is by definition, will risk the dislocation of the disciple's self; instead of a disciple, he will be a mere follower. As such he will have nothing to offer in dialogue with his master. And it cannot be repeated too often that there can be no true friendship without reciprocity.

The first quality a man must have to be recognized as a master is *prestige*. Prestige of course can be factitious, the fruit of an illusion. In this case there can be no veritable master-disciple friendship for the very simple reason that there is no master. Among true masters prestige is rooted in a real superiority even though it is not recognized by everybody. It seems to me beside the point to discuss here the prestige which certain singers and other stars enjoy in the eyes of their admirers. This is an artificially inflated prestige created for the needs of publicity; the admirers of such "masters" are in no way their disciples any more than the stars are their masters. Generally speaking, there is no real friendship between them, but at most a vague camaraderie.

It is most often intellectual or spiritual prestige which forms the basis of an existential master-discipline relationship. But it is not of the purely rational order; it is not enough to be an eminent savant or an austere ascetic to be chosen as a master. Factors of the emotional order generally play an important role in this kind of choice, and it is precisely because of this that the master-disciple relationship can blossom into friendship. It is common experience that an idea will receive a very different reception according to whether it is propounded by someone sympathetic or antipathetic. When the fishermen of Lake Tiberias abandoned without regret their boats and their nets to follow Christ in His wandering life, it was not uniquely, nor primarily, because they recognized the superior truth of His teaching. It was rather because of the mysterious influence Christ exercised on them. It was only much later, and largely under the influence of friendship which was established between them and Christ, that they came to understand His message. It was somewhat the same with Socrates and his disciples. It follows that, to learn something about Christianity or Socratic philosophy, it is more important to know the person of Christ or of Socrates than their doctrine. The latter becomes fully meaningful only when those who by virtue of an emotional impulse have become the disciple-friends of the master.

All friendship is a source of influence exercised or submitted to. This is particularly true of friendship between master and disciple. It is precisely because of fear of submitting to the influence of a stronger personality that many refuse to give themselves to a true master and become his friend. This is especially so of weak or hesitant personalities. Consciously or not, they feel that if they submit to the prestige of another and accept his influence not much of themselves will be left. Despite the affected air which they sometimes put on, those who say they have no need of a master, that they are sufficient unto themselves, are by no means strong personalities and they know it. Moreover, they are mistaken in thinking that they submit to no influence simply because they refuse to be influenced by a master. The worst form of influence is that which we submit to unconsciously. It comes from those we would under no conditions accept as masters. The truly strong man, whose self is well structured, knows well that no one is sufficient unto himself, that each of us needs the other to become himself. To meet a master who wishes to become our friend is a great opportunity in life. Thanks to him we shall be able to actualize our principal powers to the maximum. The man who has confidence in himself, far from refusing to be a disciple, freely chooses the master he believes most suited to help him become himself. If there is an art of being a master, there is also an art, scarcely less difficult, of being a disciple. The most effective masters generally began by being excellent disciples. Even Christ began by being baptized, and therefore initiated, by the Precursor.

To understand properly the nature of master-disciple friendship it is important to distinguish clearly between two kinds of influence. There is a kind of influence that enslaves those who submit to it. It emanates from a quite different kind of prestige than that possessed by the true master. Agitators and dictators like Hitler and Stalin enjoy this kind of prestige in the eyes of the masses. When we recall the collective hysteria that recently overcame one of the most civilized peoples of the world under the influence of Adolf Hitler we understand the reticence many feel, and they are not all weak characters, toward prestigious men whose influence could lead them where they have no desire to go.

Equally harmful is the influence that is derived from the more or less inflated prestige of certain intellectual leaders. We have only to recall the influence recently exercised by J. P. Sartre on an important part of French youth. Of course we do not hold Sartre's philosophy directly responsible for the "existential" crimes and debaucheries of the fifties. But the prestige of Sartrianism was much less founded on this philosophy than on the favorable publicity given to its author.

But side by side with the influence that enslaves is the influence that liberates and elevates. This is the kind of influence exercised by all masters worthy of the name. In some cases it is exercised with such discretion that the disciple himself scarcely perceives it; in retrospect he believes, in all good faith, that his spiritual evolution took place independently of all exterior influence. On the other hand, it often happens that the man who exercises the most profound influence on others is unaware of it and is the first to be surprised at the decisive role he is reputed to have played in the lives of other men. Such a person was the Curé of Ars. He sincerely believed that the crowds came to Ars to venerate the relics of St. Philomena, that it was this unknown saint who brought about the miracles and marvels which took place daily in his church.

But in most friendships between master and disciple it is normal for both parties to be aware of the currents of influence—not that the master necessarily wants to model the disciple in his own image. The master worthy of the name is rather convinced of being charged with a transcendent message and he wishes above all to communicate this message to those he loves. The disciple, for his part, is docile and disposed toward his master because he is more or less aware that the latter's prestige comes from a superior reality which transcends both of them.

The reader might ask himself whether friendship between a master and a disciple, such as we have described it, is true friendship. Have we not often insisted upon reciprocity as an essential condition for all friendship? But apparently the master only gives and the disciple receives. Even if this were always the case, emotional reciprocity would not be impossible. In a material sense, one of the friends could be rich and the other poor; one could share his riches with the other even though the latter has nothing to give in exchange—materially speaking—for what he receives. Why should it be any different in sharing spiritual goods? Friendship effectively abolishes all feeling of inferiority in him who receives; there is no place in it for calculations and equations. As for him who gives, is it not true that there is more joy in giving than in receiving? But there is more in a master-disciple friendship. These who believe, with some reason and without too much presumption, themselves to be charged with the mission of being masters toward certain other men consider it a signal honor to have disciples and, still more so, to have friends among them. The master, as a rule, is older and more experienced in life than his disciple-friends. To be surrounded by young people who love him and receive his message with enthusiasm and gratitude can only be a source of great joy to him. He finds in such friendship a fountain of youth and feels himself revived, indeed, immortal. For what he considers most important in himself, namely his message, will continue to live and survive him precisely because of the friendship of his disciples. Humanity continues to benefit by Socrates' death twenty-five centuries later precisely because of Plato and his other disciple-friends. What would have befallen the Good News of Christ without those disciple-friends who were His apostles and evangelists? Is it not because of his friends Vinoba and Nehru that Mahatma Gandhi's work has been continued among the Indian people? Of course, there can be vanity in the satisfaction an artist, a philosopher or a scholar experiences when a young admirer says "my dear master." With true masters, that is, with those who attach more importance to the message they bear than to themselves, it is rather a question of joy in being thus recognized and confirmed in their mission.

Young, educated women, more often than their male colleagues, seem disposed to friendship with a master. This is because they are generally intellectually less proud and thus recognize more readily their need to be guided. They are happy to admire and love those who have initiated them intellectually and spiritually. Friendship between an older master and a young female disciple seems to be, in our experience, the most exquisite form of friendship between men and women. The only danger is that the young woman, in her ardent desire to admire and be guided, mistakes for a master someone who does not possess the essential qualities, someone who has no transcendent message to transmit to her still-undeveloped self. Because they are less emotionally involved in their admiration for a chosen master, men generally run less risk of deceiving themselves and are, because of this, more faithful to their master-friend. But, on the other hand, many of them are content to appropriate the message of a master without establishing any emotional rapport of friendship.

XII

Communities
of friends

IT would be monstrous to speak of a community of lovers. Certainly one can perhaps observe sexual promiscuity in primitive societies or, much more often, polygamy. But there we have to do with a very low level of human development, a level at which it is not yet possible to speak of love. More than anywhere else, evolution in this domain is rectilinear, tending toward a relation of immediacy between *one* man and *one* woman. The Anarchists and some Communists who once prescribed free love for the future of humanity in the form of sexual promiscuity seriously misinterpreted the general line of human development. Even if, in accordance with their expectations, lovers no longer thought it useful to ratify their union legally, this union would nonetheless be very rigorously monogamous. We are aware, of course, that in certain highly sophisticated circles parties of sexual promiscuity are organized. But such parties have nothing in common with love and from all evidence are symptomatic of sexual perversity. A person who is psychically normal could not simultaneously love several other persons.

Friendship is a different matter. I am aware that many have a contrary opinion, maintaining that each of us can have only one "true" friend. This is because they model their conception of friendship after that of love. It is true that adolescents, particularly girls, have only one close friend in whom they confide. At this stage of emotional immaturity, as we said earlier, friendship is essentially sentimental and has much in common with the intimacy of love, although it generally excludes eroticism properly so called. These friendships are jealous like love. We are all aware of veritable dramas of jealousy in friendships between adolescent girls, sometimes ending in suicide; most often, however, they are content to speak evil of the "rival" and, indeed, to persecute her. This kind of jealous and exclusive friendship is sometimes found among adults; but then we must conclude that their emotional maturity is very inadequate, unless it is a question of more or less overt homosexuality or some other psychopathological pattern.

As we have emphasized several times, friendship by its very nature is more spiritual than carnal, although the sensual element is never absent from it. The spiritual is always necessarily rooted in the carnal. We have also seen that, unlike love, friendship does not establish immediate communication between two persons; rather, friends communicate through the mediation of something outside of them, such as an ideal or a common cause. There is nothing contradictory in the fact that we might meet several people in the service of such an ideal who are capable of becoming our friends. This is all the more possible and desirable since it is relatively rare to have perfect communion on all levels of existence with one of our friends.

I become friends with so and so, for example, because we share the same religious ideals. Human nature, however, is a very complex and, indeed, complicated reality, generally more complicated the more spiritually and emotionally developed the person is. Religious or political preoccupations do not exhaust my interests. I may also be interested in psychological and historical studies while a given friend X may be interested in something quite different, such as music, for which I have very little talent. Nothing is more normal or more desirable than that I should have a second friend with whom I can talk about my interests. It is also normal and desirable that my friend X have a musician friend. Our friendship could not be threatened by other friendships; there is no valid reason for jealousy here. Quite the contrary, by such diversification of friendship each of us can find the fulfillment of our different spiritual and emotional faculties. Our mutual friendship can only benefit. But if we remain imprisoned in a narcissistic friendship there is a strong possibility that we will soon experience dissatisfaction and disappointment as a result of not being able to communicate with a friend on the other levels we each consider important.

The more emotionally mature one is, the more "open" in Bergson's sense of the term, the more friendships one is capable of sustaining simultaneously. I know people who are or have been veritable catalysts, authentic beacons of friendship. This was, for example, the case with Emmanuel Mounier, the philosopher Jacques Maritain, the Dominican Father Maydieu and, in more remote times, a Clara Schumann. Those who do not believe in the possibility of a plurality of amicable communions sometimes say they are annoyed to hear men speak of many people as their friends. They suspect them of devaluating the beautiful word "friendship"—but they are wrong. Mounier, Maritain, Maydieu and others like them actually had many friends, not in the vague sense of many acquaintances, but in the strong and proper sense of the word. They communicated with each of their many friends *existentially*.

Nothing, moreover, prevents my friend X and my friend Y from becoming friends. They may communicate with one another on a level that I cannot. In this way true communities of friends can be formed.

Generally speaking, such communities are formed about a master, one of those catalysts of friendship we spoke of earlier. In my youth I lived intensely in such a community of friendship. The rallying point and master of this group was a celebrated revolutionary writer. We were all very different from one another in social origins, in culture and temperament since we came from different countries. But we all communicated in our common admiration for the friend-master and in that ideal of a future human and fraternal society of which he was one of the purest and most enthusiastic protagonists. And it was, indeed, a question of friendship—not mere good fellowship—among us. We all had comrades, and excellent comrades, outside of our circle of friends. The cement of this latter, as of all friendship, was of an emotional quality, but we appreciated our comrades in a more objective manner.

Many years later a group of fervent young Christians chose me as the leader of their community of friendship. I loved them all as friends and they responded in kind. With many of them this friendship will last forever, having triumphed over some twenty years of common effort. Still more important than the friendship of these young people with me was the very authentic friendship that united them one to another and, generally speaking, does so to this day. However, important social barriers sometimes separated them at the beginning. Sons and daughters of the rich lived side by side with those of very modest origins. Apart from the initial core, most of the members of the community did not know more than one or two other members before joining it. Scarcely any had been friends previously. The style and the activities of the intellectual and spiritual concerns of the community fostered very authentic and very personal friendships between all members.

Of course, not everyone can belong to a community of friends with the certainty of quickly becoming friends with all members of the group. Certain deep affinities must preexist, often unconsciously, less perhaps between all the members than between each of them and the community, for it is the latter which mediates friendship. The community I have spoken about provided abundant evidence of this. Young people who had heard of it asked one or another of us to be received into it. But many soon left because the spark of friendship was absent.

Friendship, in a community of friends, loses none of its I-Thou quality. Each of the twenty or thirty members of the group had, within it and because of it, twenty or thirty different friendships, all rigorously personal. Thanks to the dynamically spiritual and intellectual climate that prevailed in the community, the conditions for the blossoming of friendship were particularly propitious. Members confronted one another directly on essentials whereas in ordinary relationships between people it generally takes a good deal of time to rise from social banalities to authentic communication.

We noted in a previous chapter that friendship between

young people of opposite sexes scarcely seems viable
within the framework of such communities of friends.
Most of the friendships that were formed there, as well as
the relatively elevated degree of communication, offers almost certain proof that friendship cannot serve as an unconscious disguise for Eros. To be sure, it is quite possible
in such communities that love will follow upon friendship
in some cases. This, as a matter of fact, was the case in the
community of which we are speaking. But such love is
founded upon a solid basis of friendship. Twenty years
later most of the couples who met in our group still bear
the community imprint. Their love has in no way made
them selfish; the families they have founded are not at all
narcissistic but receptive and open toward the world.

Teilhard de Chardin has spoken fervently in several of
his letters of the friendly community that formed among
the scholars with whom he worked. They all belonged to
different races, countries and religions. But all were ani-
mated by the same love for knowledge and truth, all believed fervently in progress. This love and this faith enabled them to transcend their differences.

Common action—and it must be positive action, as often
as possible creative—is, in effect, the first condition for the
formation of a community of friends. It may be a question
of scientific or spiritual research; again, it might be social,
political or apostolic action. But under no circumstances
is it enough to meet at the level of leisure alone. This is
precisely what radically distinguishes a community of
friends from a group of casual companions. The first is
united by a concern for essentials, or at least for what is
subjectively essential for the members of the group. The
second, on the other hand, is founded on the unessential;

consequently, the result is not a solid and durable edifice but a simple agglomeration of juxtaposed existences.

Theoretically there should be no quantitative limit to the love of friendship. It is no mere pious metaphor when we speak of Christ, for example, as the *universal friend* of all men without exception. It is by no means excluded a priori that one day, a day we would like to be as soon as possible, humanity will conform to the optimistic vision of Teilhard de Chardin, and then each will be able to be truly the friend of all other human beings. For the moment, and undoubtedly for a long time to come, the consciences and hearts of the immense majority of men are too narrow to permit truly universal friendship. The only communities of friends possible today must be proportioned to our capacities of knowledge and love; only a few exceptional persons are able to achieve quasi-universality. Practically, and in accord with my own experience, even those who are most spiritually evolved cannot embrace more than twenty or thirty people in a community of friendship.

For, even within a community, friendship always remains an interpersonal, emotional bond. To speak, for example, of "friendly nations," as is sometimes done in official speeches, cannot mean much—at least in the present stage of human development. To be sure, we admire those Stoics who, and they were undoubtedly the first to do so, advocated friendship not only between individuals but also between peoples and states. But it seems for the moment more realistic to imitate as much as possible someone like Leibnitz, who wanted to form a world-wide community of friends, an ambition not unlike that of Teilhard de Chardin.

Let us insist once more that a plurality or a community of friends implies no weakening, to our mind, of the meaning of the word "friendship." Nor does it exclude a certain emotional hierarchy. We can certainly be closer friends with one person than with another without feeling frustrated. Christ had a preferred friend in John; Socrates too had a preferred friend. In his *Confessions* St. Augustine speaks with deep emotion of the death of a friend. He was irreplacable in Augustine's heart, but this did not prevent him from regarding his other disciples as authentic friends. The worth of friendship is, in effect, of a spiritual nature. We can therefore give "more" to one without diminishing what we give to another.

XIII

The promotion
of existence
by friendship

FROM earliest times innumerable moralists, philosophers and other thinkers and writers have affirmed that one true friend is worth infinitely more than all the riches and honors of the world. It seems, as a matter of fact, that as long as we have not lived the experience of a solid and deep friendship we can only have a pessimistic vision of human nature. Very often the decisive event in the life of a man is not the accident by which he gained a large fortune or even the success he achieves in athletic, political or intellectual competition, but rather meeting a true friend. However pleasurable be power and wealth, they contribute in a very mediocre fashion to the realization of our vocation as men; they can even become an obstacle to our fulfillment. In any case, they add nothing essential to our solitary self. The spirit of possession almost infallibly engenders avarice in the subject himself and jealousy in others. But it is beyond argument that there can be no ade-

quate fulfillment of the human person without generosity
and the forgetting of self. The friend par excellence is he
who opens himself to our generosity and who lets us share
in his. It is, therefore, primarily through this instrumentality that we can exercise ourselves in the practice of
generosity and forgetfulness of self. Communication with
a friend, that is to say with the intimate life of another,
necessarily transcends the domain of having those exchanges of an objective order which are essential to fellowship and even erotic love. It is the direct exchange of
one being with another, that is to say veritable communion
which friendship demands and encourages.

Friendship is by nature a spiritual communion; it tends
to enhance our spiritual being and riches. Yet we must
never lose sight of the fact that humans are not and never
will be pure spirits. However elevated a degree of spirituality we attain, we remain no less creatures of the flesh.
It follows that our friendships ought to be founded as
much on our carnal condition as upon our spiritual natures.
Otherwise, friendship will cease to be a concrete reality
and only an elite will succeed in achieving it. But the ordinary man, at least as much as the saints and heroes, needs
friendship as a condition of reaching the superior forms of
existence.

Friendship between those who are not "pure spirits" but
are only on the way to progressive spiritualization is certainly an intimate person-to-person dialogue; but it must
be mediated by the material world. This mediation takes
place through the common knowledge and love for something which transcends us and in which we meet one another. Here, as elsewhere, the objective and the subjective,
far from excluding one another, are mutually comple-

mentary. It is while engaged in a common work or cause, indeed, sometimes on the occasion of a ball game or other form of amusement, that we become aware of profound affinities between us and another, that we vibrate to the same rhythm and are capable of experiencing more or less identical emotions, aspirations, thoughts and intuitions. The objective reality that mediates friendship may be nature, art in any of its forms, the history of our country or of mankind, causes for the liberation of peoples or classes, philosophy, science, reading or meditation. True, these are not *causes* of friendship, but they are, nonetheless, infinitely more than simple occasions of encounter. Through their instrumentality, friendship becomes concrete and capable of promoting the existence of friends.

It is not enough for friends to realize that they know and love the same things. This is merely a preliminary phase. In order for friendship to grow and become more and more fecund it is important to cultivate this embryonic experience. Only progressively, to the degree that their coexistence intensifies and deepens, do friends acquire the unshakable certainty that they are not two solitudes chance has brought together but that the same spiritual sap circulates in them, that anything which might eventually separate them could only be a more or less unfortunate accident. The same light illuminates them; they are en route toward a similar goal even though it may regrettably not be by the same path.

We are disposed to communicate to our friend not only all we possess but also, and above all, everything that we are. It is, however, proper to friendly communion not only to give but also to receive. He who would give all to his friends but refuses to receive anything from them can scarcely benefit from friendship. We are, as a matter of fact, so constituted that the powers and riches that are in us in a state of potentiality can only with great difficulty be realized in action unless external influences set in motion the forces of inertia within us. In order for our intelligence, our heart, our faculties of action to become activated another person is necessary, someone like us and yet different from us, who sends forth a call and communicates a message to us. It may also happen that this other receives from us the message he transmitted. Friendship ripens when we are generously receptive to the message or the call that comes to us from a friend and when he is open to the message or the call we offer him. Furthermore, the call we are speaking of can scarcely be distinguished from the friend himself; in accepting him in his profound reality we accept the message of which he is the bearer.

It is in and by friendship that we experience ourselves. Through friendship we become aware of our transcendence in relation to the meanness and misery that was our lot when we were a solitary self. Because of friendship we discover a new dimension in our lives. Henceforth we see with different eyes not only our own lives but the entire universe. How marvelous to see again in the company of a friend the landscapes and paintings we had formerly admired alone, to listen with him to symphonies which formerly pleased us! We now see and hear not only with our own eyes and ears but also with those of our friend. Nor is this a question of a simple quantitative addition to the individual capacities of each. The "We" of friendship possesses its own way of seeing and hearing, a capacity of knowing and loving which transcends by far the sum of individual capacities.

The most authentic friendships always and necessarily have something other than friendship itself in view. Narcissism is not only an individual trait; there can also be a narcissistic We. As soon as friendship withdraws into the narcissistic cult of itself and has no other end than its own promotion, the contemplation of its own beauty, then the danger of failure becomes great. The "other thing" to whose service friendship consecrates itself could be the practice of art or philosophy, the fight for a better world, the cause of human brotherhood or the service of God. The more transcendent the circumstances in which friends encounter one another the more solid and beautiful will be their friendship. But at no time can we be confident that our friendship with a given person is so deep and solid that it needs no improvement. In order to endure, friendship must constantly be remade, renewed and deepened like life itself.

Life is shared between friends, each living not only his own life but also that of his friends. There must, however, be no question of appropriating the life of another as a master appropriates the life of a slave or as a dictator subjugates the masses under his influence. We make the life of a friend ours with the most total respect for his otherness. This supposes, in the first place, that we let our friend participate in exactly the same way in our life. Friendship, because of the dynamism proper to it, leads us from individual living to a state of shared existence; this implies a veritable metamorphosis of our life. Among young people such a metamorphosis is generally effected spontaneously and easily. Sometimes a simple meeting of the eyes, the exchange of a few phrases, a handshake or a small service rendered or received suffice for two people to become conscious of the birth of a mysterious communion between them and open themselves to a mutual osmosis. On the other hand, adults who have known several failures and disappointments in their emotional relationships with others only gradually overcome their mistrust and hesitations and thus become ready for a metamorphosis of their lives through friendship.

To grow and to encourage existence, friendship does not require a perfect equality with respect to culture and education, social background or intellectual achievements. An approximate equality in one or another of these respects can facilitate encounters in which the spark of friendship may be struck. There can be, and, as a matter of fact, there are authentic friendships between employers and employees, between teachers and students, between men and women, between rich and poor. However, friendship cannot fulfill its role as a promoter of existence without tending to create a certain equality between friends. In this equality, which we have called *shared existence*, all differences are dialectically transcended. In friendship we experience ourselves and the other primarily as *men*, not as rich or poor, man or woman, teacher or disciple.

Friendship enables us to become simultaneously aware of our riches and our poverty. Since generosity is the condition and the very essence of friendship, we must know what we are capable of offering our friend. We are not long in realizing that what we possess is far inferior to what we would like to give our friend. We must, therefore, continue to grow, and it will be in large part because of the generosity of our friend himself that we will be able to increase our riches, both on the level of having and on the level of being.

Friendship is not restricted to encouraging the interior treasures and beauties of friends. It must also encourage their power of action. To exist means to act and create; it is only by acting that man realizes himself, whatever the form of action be. The more he acts, the more he permits the potential of his being to actualize itself. Thought itself is nourished and takes form in action; otherwise, it would be a purely abstract kind of thinking with no hold on reality. Similarly, it is in and through action that we strengthen our capacity for loving. Friendship is capable of considerably increasing man's power of action and creation. In acting with and for each other friends can accede to a spiritually elevated level of existence which they would not have attempted alone.

The kind of activity we have in mind and which constitutes the skeleton, so to speak, of friendship has nothing in common with empty agitation or the "spontaneous activity" that Gide and his disciples encouraged. Nor does it tend to an egocentric appropriation of a certain parcel of the universe as does the Sartrian philosophy, for example, in its concept of action. Friendship is not satisfied to "do something together" but tends toward *cocreation*. By striving together to transform the world and promote the noosphere, we at the same time act creatively toward one another and develop our spiritual life.

The creative activity of friends is borne by their common hope, by their common involvement in the service of the transcendent. To the degree that this hope is strong and noble, activity will be deep and coherent and friendship will be more authentic for those who give themselves to it.

Friends act with one another, upon one another and also

for one another. Friendship carries the desire for inter-human solidarity to its highest degree. Battle comrades fight together for the triumph of a common cause. Fellow workers act in concerted effort. But neither explicitly proposes to work for one another. In friendship common work is not distinct from common action; nor is either distinct from those who act together.

There are those who are radically incapable of friendship not because of their indigence but, we might say, because of their too abundant riches. Spiritually evolved and generous men sometimes fail to make friends because they believe they have nothing to gain from others or because they think they possess everything they need. They are disposed to give but not to receive. Or, again, they may be very authoritarian types who tolerate no originality in those they love and would want to have as friends. They do not desire dialogue with others but rather a fusion, that is to say the destruction of the other's self by absorbing it in their own self. All self-affirmation in others irritates them and makes them aggressive. If they do not succeed in subjugating the other they reject him, declare friendship impossible and withdraw into a proud solipsism. Such men will never know the highest joys of friendship and will never benefit from its values. Others can in no way enrich them; nor can they give anything of existential worth to others; they merely provoke reactions of auto-defense in them.

Friendship founded on love not only tolerates and protects the personal authenticity of friends but encourages and exalts it. Nothing is more false or dangerous to friendship than the widespread prejudice that it can only thrive if the distinctive personality traits of the one are renounced in a servile effort to imitate the other. Friendship is not an anonymous sphere of repetitions and imitations. It flourishes and bears fruit only on condition that each friend become fully himself. If the other find in me nothing but a pale image or a weak echo of himself what can he expect from his friendship with me that he did not already possess?

To be capable of friendship, of spiritual communion with another, is in no way unworthy of a superior person. Quite the contrary, we may see in such a capacity the very sign of spiritual superiority and a strong personality. The mediocre are too concerned with immediate success and efficiency, too egocentric and, therefore, too little respectful of the other's personality. If they are not strong enough to dominate others then they submit servilely to them. In neither case can there be true friendship.

True friendship is possible only when we recognize and accept the differences which distinguish rather than separate us from others. Of course, there is pride and self-love in all of us that hinder the communion of friendship. We must rid ourselves of such faults. But we must be careful at the same time not to reject our distinctive personality traits. Friendship is the more beautiful and fecund insofar as each friend is truly himself. And it is by making ourselves more available to others that we become more and more ourselves. In friendship we discover and reveal what we are and, perhaps still more, what we are capable of becoming.

Of course, it is normal and necessary that one friend exercise an influence on the other. But this influence does not have as its principal end communicating our riches to the other but rather making him discover his own riches. It follows that friendship demands great discretion, much disinterest and forgetfulness of self and renunciation of self-love. We must listen to our friends, especially when they are not saying much, and be attentive to all expressions of their secret person. This proves in practice to be much more difficult than giving what we already possess or receiving what the other presently has to offer. If we take this easy way out we will be incapable of authentic friendship.

XIV

The finitude
of all that
is human

AFTER having spoken at such length about the value of friendship, about the fidelity and spirituality that characterize it, I begin this last chapter with some hesitation. Yet, taking into account the eminently practical objective of this book, it would be dangerous to court illusions. Certainly friendship promises us joy and unveils the meaning of our own existence, as well as that of others. But however perfect friendship may be, it is no more exempt from the risk of fissure and finitude than other form of interhuman communication.

It is never absolutely certain that even the most beautiful friendship will not end in failure and disappointment. The friend with whom we think we have realized the most total union is susceptible to being solicited by other calls which may prove to be irreconcilable with the form our friendship has taken. It may evolve in a direction impossible to follow. It is therefore to be feared that little by little the friend will become alienated from me, that the bonds of our friendship will weaken and finally break.

The death of a friend is without doubt the least catastrophic end of a true friendship. We have only to recall the immortal pages in which Montaigne praises his deceased friend Étienne de la Boétie to be convinced that, at least in privileged cases, friendship is capable of surviving death. I frequently look at the portrait of my old friend Emmanuel Mounier, dead now some fourteen years, which hangs in my office; I feel that he is as present as during the time of our endless conversations years ago. Without speaking of Christ and His friends, we can see that friendship between master and disciple, as the example of Socrates particularly illustrates, is very capable of triumphing victoriously over the trial of death. One can even have very authentic friendship for a master long since deceased and whose disciple one became through the mediation of his work. Thus did Christ have innumerable friends in countries and times far removed from Palestine at the time of the Roman Empire.

A prolonged physical separation is more trying for a friendship. Of course, friendship survives such separations in many cases; friends can meet after ten or twenty years as though they had parted only yesterday. This is done more easily when the exchange of an intensive correspondence has kept the dialogue alive. It is highly regrettable in this respect that the precipitated rhythm of modern life prevents the exchange of those long and intimate letters that was formerly the custom. Today we are content to pass on news but no longer have the time to converse by means of letters. There is, therefore, a greater danger than formerly that physical separation will gradually lead to the separation of souls. The development of each undergoes different influences, conditions of life and relationships; the result can be such a spiritual estrangement between friends that they will no longer be able to renew their dialogue. In this case, it is better not to force the issue and at least to retain fond memories of the dead friendship. As for the former friend himself, let us be content to count him henceforth among our good comrades.

Not infrequently a friendship between two men ends because of a woman. Before marrying John, Martha had been engaged to his friend George. The latter broke off the engagement for reasons that were perfectly honest and acceptable. Martha then married John, whom she loved sincerely. Yet she could not suppress feelings of bitterness toward George until she succeeded in bringing about a final rupture between John and his lifelong friend. It goes without saying that it was a very painful experience for John and George to have their friendship ruined by external influences. But at least they could retain feelings of esteem and affection for one another since there had been no deception on the part of either.

The opposite can also happen, that is to say, a friendship between two women may end because of a man. Nicole and Marie were inseparable friends from childhood. Their friendship continued after Nicole's marriage. Her husband was jealous of this relationship, having gotten the impression that his wife communicated better with her friend than with himself. Marie was attractive to him, and he employed all his knowledge of women to conquer her. He succeeded after a time and arranged to have his wife discover him and Marie together in highly suspect circumstances. Needless to say, this was the end of the friendship between the two women. Nicole was aware that her husband seduced Marie for reasons of jealousy. She bore him some ill will but soon forgave him for his unconventional behavior. But she never pardoned her friend, even though she knew that she was more a victim than a guilty party. This kind of reaction is fairly general among women; men, on the other hand, react very differently in similar situations. They blame their wives and forgive the friend much more readily.

The worst disappointment is the betrayal of a friendship by a friend. It is not difficult for us to imagine with what sorrow Christ must have said to Judas, who had come to betray Him, "Friend, for what purpose hast thou come?" The tragedy of Christ's life would have been infinitely less if He had been betrayed to the Sanhedrin and Pilate by one of His enemies among the Pharisees. It is not our intention to analyze here the psychological process which made a traitor of this friend. What is certain is that there will always be Judases in this world.

It sometimes happens that men identify so totally with a "cause" that they take it as a personal betrayal when one of their friends leaves the said cause. Almost all ex-Communists have been saddened by this experience. Nothing authorizes us to doubt the authenticity of the friendships they formed with members of the party. But when—say, on the occasion of Stalin's purges or the bloody suppression of the Hungarian and Polish uprisings in 1956— their consciences directed them to leave the Communist party, even their best friends among those who remained faithful denounced them and broke all bonds of friendship with them. According to them the "apostates" had betrayed them, as well as the party.

Within Christianity the spirit of tolerance has made great progress in recent times. I know priests of unquestionable fidelity to the Church who remain on close terms of friendship with former confrères who have left the Church's service. We may see in this a sign of psychological and emotional maturity.

We have no reason to suppose that all friendships which for one reason or another failed were false friendships. Here, as elsewhere, we must recognize that everything human is fragile, more or less fragile depending upon the individuals and their situations. It would be dangerous to form a too inhumanly elevated idea of friendship. Many, in this case, would not dare attempt it and would thus renounce one of the deepest sources of joy in this life. On the other hand, there is always an element of dissatisfaction in even the most successful friendships. We would like to share everything with our friends and keep nothing for ourselves. But experience proves that every human being possesses a central core that is so intimate that it is practically incommunicable. Consequently, even in the most beautiful friendships there remains the more or less obscure feeling that we are not understood and loved absolutely, that we ourselves do not understand and love our friends "all the way."

Nonetheless, its imperfections and limitations notwithstanding, friendship represents one of the most precious values of the human condition. It is certainly worth the effort to commit ourselves courageously to the experience of friendship.